Holidays

and

Holy Days

The Society of Women Writers WA Inc

A catalogue record for this book is available from the National Library of Australia

ISBN-13: 978-1-922343-03-1

Acknowledgments

The Society of Women Writers WA Inc would like to acknowledge the following members for their collective efforts in bringing members' writing to publication: the Book Editors Club – Jan Altmann, Lynne Cairns, Sue Colyer, Helen Iles, Val McCabe, Marilyn Rainer, Shirley Rowland, and June Smith; the anthology Receiving Officer, editor and book designer Helen Iles, and proof reader Maria Bonar. We thank each of you for your role in bringing *Holidays and Holy Days* to fruition.

Contents

Foreword

October, and many may already be thinking of Christmas and planning the gifts they must buy for family and friends. The good news is that another fascinating anthology is about to be launched in time for your Christmas list. That anthology, *Holidays and Holy Days*, is written by the talented ladies of the Society for Women Writers WA and consists of a great variety of short stories and poems.

The holidays, which are renewed memories or new experiences, take us across the world. We go to a beautiful, peaceful place in Greece where we will write our planned 'bestseller'. We travel to Israel, Japan, Zambia, Amsterdam and many more places, but we find that holidays are not always what we expect. Some are more fun and will be long remembered; others are memorable for different reasons. One writer summarises beautifully, "In travel as in life, no matter how much wonder and excitement you encounter, crises punctuate the enjoyment. Perhaps they play as important a role as the pleasure, separating the spectacular and amazing by unforgettable dramas."

We search for the true meaning of Christmas, as we reflect on past joys and blessings with family and friends. But we are saddened at the blatant commercialism these holy days have become as we are urged to spend – spend – spend. How sad that for some, Christmas is now a "noisy commercial cardboard ritual". There is so much more meaning to Christmas and those holy days.

It was great to read of and remember our joy and wonder as children. We are reminded of how fairies and angels become part of life as they weave their magic spells through our lives – and Santa arrives just in time to cope with our requests! What a shame when those dreams of childhood are shattered, and we discover it was Mum and Dad who provided that big teddy bear.

The stories and poems in this anthology are vibrant and full of interesting thoughts and ideas with plenty of humour throughout. What a shock to find you are not alone as you planned but will share the dream cruise with a friend!

My congratulations to all the contributors to this little anthology *Holidays and Holy Days*, and I trust many will find it in their Christmas stocking this year! Maybe Santa will have a copy for you as he arrives on his motorbike!

Patron Ruth Reid

Cruising with Escher

They must know about those images
by Escher, of birds becoming fish,
and fish becoming birds;
those gannets, cruising, white-winged,
yellow-breasted, on the blue of the sky,
with me cruising below on the South China Sea.

They wheel under and over,
silently circle their memories, far from land;
willing their insistent, anxious spirits
out into the sky and the water;
light above and dark below.

Clouds drift, unconcerned.
The secret-whispering wind
gathers and spreads their thoughts;
soaring, swooping, ceaselessly searching,
beseeching the heavens above
and questioning the water below.

One breaks.
Wings fold.
In perfect harmony eyes, beak
and shuddering tail
plunge towards the unknown.
Touching the waves, it soars upwards again,
just before breaking the water.
Another follows.
A wave reaches and splashes.
There is no return.

Sky and water interchange.
White birds darken and disappear;
swim, and then lighten again.
The spaces between become
birds swimming and fish flying,
on the same mysterious quest.

What do the depths reveal?
The mystery of their metamorphosis?
Only the water knows.

Escher, Sea and Sky.

Jan Altmann

Reflections in Monet's Garden

In waves they surge, slow, recede and surge again.
Cars, trucks and tourist buses zoom and drone,
tear into the green and gold serenity
of the softly scented crepuscular air.

Then, as if by magic, the urgency subsides.
Trees in green, gold and purple gothic arches
rise and draw me into the slowly fading, vaulted sky;
reach ever upwards
to the silver clouds and the ether beyond,
gateways to that indefinable otherness.

Symmetry is everywhere.
A matching pair of green bridges paint their arches
over the water,
offering safe passage
from one side to the other.

They promise pathways across realities,
and then repeat themselves in the moving arches
of the trees that downward bend in shimmering waves;
touch the deep, everlasting water,
and the lilies that Monet called his Nympheas;
those pink and yellow spirits floating
amongst the leaves of deepest green.

Light, descends in rays;
casting leaves and flowers into sprays and shadows
that glow deep into the water.
Symmetry breathes a change
that images no change, but a perfect reflection.
Time and permanence, discord and concord
ascend and descend.
Symmetry is everywhere,
transcends itself,
becomes a moving image of eternity.
Light fades and the traffic resumes.

Jan Altmann

Limnisa: Seclusion and Silence –a True Writer's Retreat in Greece

Birdsong and the constant lulling sound of the waves; the taste of freshly baked apple cake and good coffee; the salty tang of the sea, rosemary and jasmine perfume the air...

This was my second trip to the Writer's Retreat at Limnisa in Greece, owned by Mariel Hacking and Phillip Wooderson. The house is by the shore on the Methana peninsula, with the islands of Aegina and Angistri across the water. It is spacious and airy with five bedrooms, all with sea views. A fully-equipped tent in the garden is available for the writer on a budget.

Phillip is English. Mariel is from the Netherlands and speaks Dutch, English, Greek, French, Spanish, German and Italian. There were ten guests at the retreat, from Paris, Berlin, Glasgow, Amsterdam, Oslo, Cumbria and Western Australia. English was the *lingua franca* around the dining table.

Six of us had previously visited Limnisa. Most of us came with specific projects to work on, away from the demands of work or domestic responsibilities.

Limnisa is a place of beauty and tranquility. Inside, there are paintings, objects d'art and quirky beachcomber finds on display; cupboards full of books in English, Dutch and other languages, from Shakespeare or Margaret Atwood, to the Art of Frida Kahlo. Outside, there are graceful arches running along the wide veranda and more delightful objects to discover in little niches and corners. Even the paved areas of coloured stone are lovely. There is no lack of inspiration for the writer.

The terraced garden has lemon, fig and tamarisk trees, hibiscus, bougainvillea, grape vines, cacti, herbs and colourful pots of flowers. A stone wall marks the lower perimeter of the garden from the shoreline of volcanic black pebbles. Shaded seating areas are built onto the wall, which is topped by unusual rock sculptures.

Further up the slope, there are hammocks and garden benches. There are hidden nooks and crannies everywhere and writers are free to work where they choose – on terraces, under pergolas, on a natural rock seat, or indoors and they are encouraged to move tables, chairs, cushions and umbrellas to suit themselves.

An early riser, I had the veranda to myself each morning and had breakfast while watching a pair of swallows catch insects to feed the three chicks in their nest, high up on the wall. By the time I left, the chicks were crowding the nest and the busy parents had almost completed a second, bigger one in the opposite corner. Shoals of fish splashed and leapt out of the water. There was a placid rhythm and routine to each day.

Silent time was strictly observed each morning until lunch was served. Afternoons were more relaxed, for swimming, walking or cycling, but they were quiet too. There were few distractions for those who wanted to concentrate on writing all day. Lunch and dinner times were very convivial, particularly the evenings when writers relaxed with a few glasses of wine. Meals were served buffet style and were varied and delicious, with appetising aromas drifting from the kitchen for a couple of hours before the dinner bell summoned us to the table. We were like Pavlov's dogs, salivating at the sound of the bell, wondering what delights Mariel or Phillip had cooked for us.

The menu was vegetarian, based on Greek and Mediterranean cooking and made with fresh, organically-grown local produce. Tea, coffee and fresh fruit were always available. There was a small charge for beer, local wine, ouzo and soft drinks.

Saturday night was taverna night, with dinner in the nearby villages of Agios Georgios or Agios Nikolaos. Prices were very reasonable at €13 per head.

Mariel held a yoga session by the sea before breakfast every day. Each week, she organised a film night, a silent walk and two guided meditation sessions at sunset. There was a literary night after dinner midweek for those who wished to share their writing. These optional activities were included in the cost of the retreat.

Excursions offered were a round trip of the Methana peninsula including the volcano for €25 which included a drink in the picturesque village of Vathi, overlooking the marina. Or for €15, a guided walk to Profiti Ilias, the highest point of Methana, to see the ancient remains of settlements and the chapel at the top. The views are magnificent, but you have to be fit for the 45 minute walk.

Limnisa is a place of seclusion and privacy – a true retreat. The nearest village is a 15 minute walk or 7 minute bike ride. Bikes are available free for guests to use. There are no shops in the village.

Wi-fi is not available at Limnisa, although some guests arranged their own wi-fi access on their mobile phones. I was content not to have the temptation.

There are no group workshops to lure or distract, although Phillip offers one-to-one personal workshops or manuscript consultations for retreat participants for an additional charge.

Socialising with other writers at lunch times and in the evening was a bonus and a welcome break. I am not fluent in languages other than English, but I am always pleasantly surprised when overseas to find that my schoolgirl French and university Italian still float somewhere in my subconscious. Synapses start firing off and often the word or phrase I'm looking for springs to mind when needed.

I spent eleven nights at Limnisa and finished several pieces of writing that had been sitting on my desktop for quite some time, including completing a short story and converting it into a play. Apart from the lunch break, I worked on my writing projects from after breakfast until 5 or 6pm. I was pleased at the number of items I crossed off my list.

I regularly attend writer's retreats. Limnisa is different in that it offers the opportunity to be totally immersed in your writing projects each day in beautiful, inspiring surroundings without the distraction of background chatter, workshops or wi-fi. There is time for socialising with other writers, for exchanging ideas, receiving feedback at the literary dinner and for new writers to be nurtured by more experienced writers, but these are evening pursuits. The daytime silence is perfect for the flow of writing and ideas. Optional excursions are carefully scheduled at the end of the week, when participants have had several days to establish a routine, to produce a volume of work and perhaps be ready for a break, sightseeing around the peninsula. Writing is a sedentary occupation, but the morning yoga session helps bring body and mind together with exercise, breathing and meditation, improving muscular and postural strength and flexibility. Mariel is trained in foot reflexology and reiki treatments, so most of us booked a relaxing session with her during our stay. All meals are provided, so you don't have to think about food preparation or cooking. The cost of the retreat is very reasonable considering participants are looked after, body and soul.

There are writer's retreats at Limnisa each May and September. On both my trips to Greece, I have visited another Greek Island, for a change of pace and scenery after attending the retreat at Limnisa. In 2016, I visited Hydra and in 2018 I spent four days on Spetses. It's an excellent way to have an overseas holiday while working on writing projects – and travelling provides a whole range of new experiences and topics to write about.

Maria Bonar

A version of this article was published on 'BootsnAll' One-Stop World Travel Guide Website on 6 July 2018

A "Ducky" Holiday

Four little ducks went out one day
Over the hills and far away
Two on motorbikes and two pushbikes - Yay!
What fun on a farm on a holiday

They raced up the hill and in their play
Made signs for the track – but not all day
Helped Grandpa 'n Dad in the yards they say
Then over the hills but not far away,

They swarm into the house for a snack
Drinks and "biccies" under attack
Then race up the hill and down the track
But Grandma knew they'd all be back.

Six days of noise, laughter and fun
Country cousins all at a run
All so busy in the bright spring sun
Four sleepy heads when day is done.

Two little ducks went home one day
Over the hills and far away
Then the other two went later that day
Grandma knew that they couldn't stay

So when Grandma said "Quack, quack, quack"
Sadly no little ducks came back.

Two of them had little pocket "two-ways" for safety, and one was calling another "The Duck" – hence this poem!

As some may not be familiar with the little Pre-Primary Singing game of diminishing numbers I will explain.

"Five little ducks went out one day
Over the hills and far away
Mother Duck then said "Quack, quack, quack"
But only four little ducks came back."

and so on until -

"One little duck went out one day
Over the hills and far away
Mother Duck then said "Quack, quack, quack
But NO little ducks came back."

Philippa Bostock

A Holiday to Remember

At 7.05 pm, on Tuesday, the 27th of December 1955, I boarded the 'Westland', a long train drawn by a great, puffing steam locomotive, at Perth Railway Station, along with seventeen other excited teenagers. We were the Fremantle Ladies Highland Pipe Band, heading off for the band's very first trip east.

I'd joined the band when I was fourteen, and like most of the other pipers, was taught to play the bagpipes by the band's founder, Mister Mac. Most pipers were men and a girls' band was a bit of a novelty, so we were very popular with the public. The music of the bagpipes has been heard in Australia since the early days of white settlement, because when Scottish settlers came to the Australian colonies, they brought with them their own distinctive traditions and culture.

We arrived at Kalgoorlie next morning, to be welcomed by members of the town's Scottish community, who took us on a tour of the town, after which we changed into our uniforms and marched down the main street playing our bagpipes and drums. Of course, the Eastern Goldfields climate is much hotter than Perth, and it was midsummer, so after parading through town clad in heavy kilts, plaids and long socks, we were melting.

We'd heard a lot from the locals about their new swimming pool, the first Olympic sized pool in the state, so that's where we headed, quickly changing into our swimsuits. When my best friend, the band's tallest girl, jumped in, I followed her, but I had only ever swum in the sea, except for a few swimming lessons in the Swan River, which is pretty salty in summer. Fresh water was something else. Without the buoyancy lent by salt, I went straight to the bottom. Spluttering and gasping, I climbed up my friend and clung to her while I caught my breath. That is my most lasting memory of that visit to Kalgoorlie.

On the Thursday, we were driven out to the Transcontinental Railway depot to board the train for the east. That was the first time I crossed the Nullarbor Plain, though I've done it many times since, by car and caravan, or campervan. But travelling on those old trains was unlike modern travel experience, and crossing from east to west on the Indian Pacific was a real disappointment. It never felt like a 'real' train. Despite the rattling of the old carriages over the sleepers, there was a magic to the old trains that held echoes of the dangers and hardships suffered by the men who laid those rails in the outback.

Late on Friday, we pulled into Port Pirie station in South Australia, to be welcomed by members of the local Caledonian Society. After playing a selection of tunes at the station, we boarded another train for Adelaide.

Next morning, when we arrived at Adelaide station, we were greeted by the sound of the bagpipes. It was our tutor and founder playing the tune he had composed and named for the band. During the day, we were entertained by members of Adelaide bands, before catching a train to Mt Gambier in the evening. During the overnight trip in sit-up carriages, few of us got much sleep and all arrived about 8am next morning, tired and very cold.

We were staying at the homes of members of the Blue Lake Ladies Pipe Band, who welcomed us to Mt Gambier to the sound of pipes and drums. It was a free day, so most of us caught up with a bit of sleep. The low mid-summer temperatures came as quite a shock, but we all had a lovely time at Mt Gambier, despite the cold and rain. Even at New Year, it was so cold that some of our woollen band socks were called on to double as bed-socks.

Then it was New Year's Eve and the Highland Games began. It

was a great experience for us girls to meet members of the many bands from other States, and to listen to the playing of top musicians. During the day, four pipers and two drummers competed in a miniature band contest, and several members entered solo contests, while our highland dancers won trophies.

In the evening, we joined with the Blue Lake Ladies Pipe Band and marched through the streets to a New Year dance. There were plenty of nice boys in town who liked girls in kilts, so we were all busy dancing until 11.30, when we joined all the other bandspeople to form a 'massed band' that paraded through the streets to 'pipe in' the New Year. It seemed that the whole town was out on the streets celebrating Hogmanay, the Scottish New Year, and the atmosphere was wonderful.

The Mt Gambier scenery and weather were very much what I imagined Scotland to be like, and the position of the town near the lake, with hills all around, meant that the music of the pipes echoed across the valley all through the night. Few of us got much sleep that night and crawled into our beds at dawn, exhausted, exhilarated but sober (unless some older girls bent the band rules).

New Year's Day was spent sleeping in, then picnicking with our hosts. On the 2nd of January, the Highland Games continued and we competed in the Street March Competition, before leaving for Adelaide in the evening. Members of the local bands came to the station to play the train out.

Arriving back in Adelaide at 7.45 am, after another overnight trip, we were met by photographers and reporters from the Adelaide Advertiser. Like the Western Australian press, they got people's names and other details wrong.

In Adelaide, we stayed at the Migrant Hostel in Elder Park, near the Torrens River, right next to the swimming pool, which was fortunate, as the weather was very hot. I'd got used to swimming pool water by then. It was dormitory-style accommodation and not very luxurious, with boring food. The main courses weren't too bad, if a bit uninteresting, but the sweets mainly consisted of runny and absolutely tasteless custard. After a while none of us bothered with the second course. However, we soon made up for the lack by consuming large amounts of toffee-coated peanuts and other sweets from a confectionary shop in Rundle Street.

Our time in Adelaide was a wonderful experience for most of us who'd never been out of Western Australia before. The local bands and Scottish community made a great fuss of us, organizing events and tours. One night, we played at the Trotting Ground and on Sunday paraded through town twice to attend different church services.

We visited Parliament House and the Adelaide Advertiser office and played at a concert at the Memorial Drive Tennis Courts. On the 9th, we were taken on a tour of the Barossa valley, and the following day paraded through Adelaide to the Town Hall for a Civic Reception, where we were given the keys of the city. On another day, a recording was made of the band playing.

It was exciting meeting so many girls and young men who shared our love of the pipes. We were particularly taken with the young chaps of the Adelaide Caledonian Pipe Band who, like us, wore the Macgregor tartan. However, the two girls who met their future husbands in Adelaide chose non-bandsmen, my best friend being swept off her feet by a very persistent young Scotsman.

Coming home was, for me and the few others who weren't seasick, the highlight of the trip. In those days several major shipping lines had regular runs to Australia, bringing migrants from Britain and Europe, and there were often empty berths between the eastern states and Western Australia, so it was possible to book for the interstate trip. We sailed back to Fremantle in the P&O ocean liner *Strathnaver*. The liner left Port Adelaide at 11 pm on the 17th of January 1956. The band was given a marvellous send-off, with the ship being piped out by the Adelaide pipe bands.

Few of the girls had any experience of sea travel, and most were more or less seasick. I was one of the lucky ones. As long as I could escape from our four-berth cabin way down on G Deck, and get up into the fresh air, I could survive. At one time there were only five of us up and about, though we were able to scrape a band together to put on a performance for passengers and crew on the last evening. The ship docked at Fremantle early on the 21st and was piped into the wharf by Pipe Major Robert Sinclair of the Fremantle Pipe Band. For those of us who weren't sick, it was a lovely experience.

Many years later, after the band had sadly ceased to exist, I was asked to write its history and was able to relive some of those great experiences. But why did this group of young women, who had entertained the Western Australian public for nearly fifty years, fade away? Back when it all started in the late 1940s, there were no women's bands in the state, while the men jealously guarded their organizations from incursions by females. To many of the older generation, the idea of girls playing pipes and wearing the kilt was unthinkable, so the women's bands were born. By the late 1980s, however, gender restrictions had broken down in most walks of life. Now girls were welcome in formerly male-only bands, and could even join the Australian Army reserve pipes and Drums, originally the band of the 16th Battalion Cameron Highlanders and actually get paid for playing bagpipes. That was something we could only dream of in my day.

Lynne Cairns

Santa's Gift

People still called them Koala bears
I'd seen a toy one, God knows where
For toys were scarce and very dear
In those war years

And then I met that strange old man
Whose magic powers mean he can
Grant my wishes, so I was told
Well, I was only five years old

And still believed in Santa then
And fairies, mermaids and mermen
And so I whispered in his ear
Please, I'd like a teddy bear

So when I woke on Christmas morn
In the dim, dark light of early dawn
I saw there, sitting on my bed
A great big, furry, ginger Ted

Now I knew that Santa didn't come
And that came from Dad and Mum
Who never had a lot to spend
But hoped my lack of toys to mend

Poor unloved teddy had no real name
in my small mind, he bore the blame
For my unconscious, silent grief
On losing my naïve child's belief

Until much later came a day
With only my little brother to play
At cowboys riding round their ranches
On a fallen tree's bark-free branches

We found that Teddy could play a part
In whatever game we chose to start
Sheriff, or baddy to shoot - Bang! Bang!
A silent member of our gang

Lynne Cairns

The Trouble With Modern Holidays

In Australia, our oldest, well established holidays were Christian holy days. They have their origins in the story of Jesus Christ. Christians celebrate his birth at Christmas, and his death and alleged resurrection at Easter. Many nominal Christians, however, aren't regular churchgoers, perhaps only attending on these significant days, or not at all.

So for many of us, the celebration has moved far from the church. What remains is a celebration of family, which unfortunately has been exploited by commercial interests, so now, from somewhere in spring, we are immersed in Christmas music, Santa figures, Christmas trees, tinsel and the persistent voices telling us to spend, spend, spend, because our children might be disadvantaged if they don't possess the latest brightly-coloured plastic rubbish.

Most children have a great time on the day, especially the little ones who still believe that all this largesse comes from that magic old man named Santa, and not out of the pockets or credit cards of their parents. Some really disadvantaged children must think it strange that Santa brings so much to others, while older children are confused that parents have money to spend at Christmas that they don't have for the rest of the year.

For many adults, however, Christmas seems to have deteriorated into an opportunity to get drunk and eat too much, while Easter has become a Festival of Chocolate. Cadburys and the other chocolate-makers must be laughing all the way to the bank. Even eggs have only a tenuous connection to the Bible story, bunnies don't appear anywhere in there either, and even the name Easter has pagan, pre-Christian origins. All these things are part of an age-old celebration of spring in the northern hemisphere. Here, of course it is autumn. Perhaps we are celebrating the first rains and the new grass springing after rain. Of course we have bunnies, too many of them, with us all year. Ask the farmers.

The trouble is most of us are all so well off that there are very few things that we can give or receive that are special treats. All the good food and drinks are available to us all year round, hence all the frightening obesity we see around us.

When I was a child, ice cream, soft drinks, chocolate, Christmas pudding, fruitcake and a roast chicken dinner were special treats. Now, these are everyday food, plus crayfish, prawns and exotic fruit. What can we turn on for a special meal? Strangely, what seems to have happened is that chefs have turned back the clock to make the everyday dishes of the past, like stews and casseroles in their many forms, be seen as exciting new dishes.

Perhaps, we could also go back to the holiday customs of earlier times, when children were happy with one big present and a few extra sweets, and when families could get together to enjoy each other's company, without an excess of food and alcohol.

Lynne Cairns

The Last Christmas Tree

Gordon's small hand tugged at his mother's as they walked along the pavement. At first, Anne Chalmers didn't respond. At the second, more urgent tug, she turned to see a look of expectation on her son's face as he gazed along the road ahead. Set back from the edge of the pavement was the temporary, fenced enclosure stacked with small fir trees to be sold as Christmas trees.

'Not today, Gordon,' she said, walking a little faster and holding his hand tightly. Seven-year-old Bertie skipped along to catch up.

'Why not today, Momma?' Gordon's breath made a small cloud in the cold air.

'Not today because we must hurry to visit Grandma Verl before Christmas at the seniors' village.' Frowning, Anne worried how she would to explain to the children that she couldn't afford a Christmas tree this year.

'Maybe tomorrow, Momma?' Gordon interrupted her thoughts, pulling gently on her hand again.

'Hurry along now, Gordon. Roberta, stay beside me along this busy road.'

Mother and children hurried on to morning tea with Grandma Verl. The children smiled at the large plate of cookies and sparkling sodas. Anne relaxed at the children's delight. She sat back, a tentative smile softened her face. She sipped her coffee slowly, enjoying the quiet moment with memories evoked by the last of Grandma's fine china cups with their mismatched saucers from another home.

'We're getting a Christmas tree, Gramma Verl!' Bertie and

Gordon bounced up and down excitedly.

'That's lovely, my dears,' replied Grandma Verl, who started a long story about decorating Christmas trees when she was a small girl. Bertie and Gordon no longer listened, their eyes filled with the image of the very large and colorfully decorated Christmas tree, sparkling across the communal lounge of Grandma's senior residence. They were mesmerized by the twinkling red and green lights, and the large packages stacked around its trunk.

On the long walk home, the children continued to ask when they might have their Christmas tree. Anne hesitated to give them a clear answer. In desperation, she finally said, 'Maybe on Wednesday.'

The children squealed out as they passed by the charity tree sellers and the trees again.

'We're getting a tree on Wednesday! We're getting a tree on Wednesday!'

The tree sellers, in colourful lumber jackets, looked up from their steaming coffee cups and, smiling, called back, 'See you on Wednesday, then!'

The next days passed slowly for the children. Every day Gordon asked if the day was Wednesday, and every day Roberta answered him maternally, 'Today isn't Wednesday, it's Saturday!' Every time Gordon was crest fallen.

Anne looked at the children's faces. The shadow of sadness in those innocent faces was softened by a glimmer of anticipation. Their father, Dan, left six months ago and wouldn't be coming home again. Dealing with their father's absence in the weeks approaching Christmas was particularly hard. Dan always managed to cut a fir sapling from the woods. They all enjoyed decorating the little tree; laughing and teasing each other about what each might find under the tree on Christmas morning. When Dan, as well as many other men, were dismissed from their jobs in the difficult economic times, Anne and Dan could no longer afford the mortgage. With no house and little prospect of work, their small family broke apart under the strain. Dan went in search of work, leaving silence where there once was laughter.

Now, just weeks before Christmas, Anne was tired and anxious about this first Christmas without her husband, the father of her children. She worried about managing on the small income from her part-time job at the local gas station. The small change saved each week was just enough money for some special treats for the children, she thought, but it wouldn't stretch to the price of a charity Christmas tree. She almost smiled at the irony of that thought: 'I'm a charity myself this year!' she said out loud.

Finally, Anne gave in as she counted the dollars in her savings wallet. If she bought the children just one new book between them and only one new pair of sox each, she believed that she might just have enough money. And with the two dollars 'to buy something for the children' from Grandma Verl, she might be able to afford the smallest of charity Christmas trees. Closer to Christmas the price of a tree might be cheaper than the few spare dollars in her wallet. As she watched the children making paper chains and stars to decorate the anticipated tree, her decision was made.

Wednesday arrived. Two days before Christmas Day. The excited children were warmly dressed in snow-suits. Anne pulled her woollen scarf tight around her ears. They set off early to walk to the charity tree stall on Front Street. The bright day was cold. No more snow had fallen overnight, and the sky was blue. The small family stepped carefully on the icy pavement not yet cleared by the shop owners along the street.

As they turned a corner on to Front Street, a man was walking away from the tree stall with a small fir tree over his shoulder. It was the last one. The charity Christmas tree enclosure was empty. Anne, Gordon and Bertie stood motionless, mouths open, staring into the empty space. Just a few days ago the enclosure was almost full of perfectly shaped, green fir trees of the children's dreams. The tree seller in the red jacket walked over to the trio standing like statues at the gate.

'Sorry, Ma'am, that was our last tree. No more comin' in now before Christmas! Sorry, kids.' He turned away to continue packing.

Slowly, Anne and the children also walked away, heads low, shoulders drooping.

'I hope that man has little children who will love our tree,' said Bertie thoughtfully, looking back in the direction of the last tree. She tried to be grown up and not cry for that little fir tree.

'I would love it better!' piped up Gordon. 'And now Dadda won't be coming home.'

He snatched his hand away from Anne's attempt to hold it. Anne's chest was heavy with heartache for the children's disappointment, and for her own loneliness.

'You know what we'll do now we're in town,' Anne tried to say cheerfully. 'Let's go to the park to look at all the different living trees. I always think it's sad to cut down those beautiful little fir trees. We enjoy them for a few days at Christmas, then throw them away.'

Bertie and Gordon shuffled after their mother in resigned silence. Their faces creased with sadness, the image of their tree walking away down the street still in their eyes.

Entering the park, they gasped at the vista of some tall trees reaching into the bright blue sky, as other trees bowed low under the weight of wet snow. The children's spirits lifted in the beauty of the park sparkling under the bright winter sun. The summer lawn was covered with a white carpet of snow. The paths were obscured, only marked by foot prints of someone walking a dog; a big dog, too, by the size of the prints.

'No snow balls!' called their mother, as the children ran to jump in the thickest of snow drifts.

Along the path deciduous trees were trimmed by ribbons of snow piled along their barren branches. In contrast, the evergreen firs and cedars, garbed in a glaze of snow, glistened in the morning sun. Gordon and Bertie ran to a large fir tree to stretch their arms around its girth of rough bark.

'Was this once a little tree that has grown up?' asked Gordon in wide-eyed innocence.

'Yes. It may be 100 years old,' replied Anne.

'Look, here is a poor broken tree.' Gordon rushed to the large broken branch dangling from a big leaf maple tree. A few large brown leaves clung to smaller twigs.

'Poor tree!' replied Anne. 'I think the snow came early for this tree. The weight of snow clinging to its big leaves was too heavy for this weaker branch.'

Anne walked over to the tree and stroked the broken branch. A symmetrically shaped smaller branch broke away easily from the main branch as Anne gave it a sharp tug. Her eyes brightened as she remembered reading about alternative Christmas trees in an old magazine in a waiting room somewhere.

'Look here, kids! I think we can make this branch our Christmas tree.' The children ran to her in expectation.

'How, Momma?' they asked in unison.

'Well, we could paint it white. Fix it in a planter. You could decorate it with your paper chains and stars.'

'Could we, Momma? Could we?' both children asked again in unison. 'No one else would have a tree just like ours.' Bouncing up and down the children made large deep boot prints in the snow.

The small procession, happier now, made its way home, gently carrying the broken maple branch, soon to become a Christmas tree. They trimmed its small branches, and painted it white, using up some old house paint found in the basement. Anne secured the tree in an old red planter.

Tears filled Anne's eyes as she listened to the happy laughter from the lounge as the children decorated the tree with their paper chains and paper stars. Memories of those other Christmases came back strongly; a mix of joy and heartbreak. Anne busied herself planning treats for Christmas Day: perhaps some bacon for breakfast and cookies to go with milk after supper.

On Christmas morning, Gordon and Roberta rushed to their special Christmas tree. They found small presents under the tree, wrapped in colorful old magazine pages – a book each, and a package of sox each: two pairs with blue stripes for Gordon, and two pairs of yellow spotted sox for Roberta. A small brown paper package was tagged 'Momma'. The children had pooled their pocket money to buy a special lavender soap for Anne. Anne gathered the children into her arms as she wished them a happy Christmas, just managing to place a kiss on each head as they pulled away to look at their books

'Dad, you got it wrong again!' said the small boy. 'Last time you told me the story, you said you got green sox.'

'Well, Gordie, it's hard to remember all the details after 25 years. I was about your age when my mother, your Grandma Annie, made us that most beautiful Christmas tree. We didn't throw out that tree after 12 days. We kept it in the basement, and every Christmas it came to life again for us. We would decorate it about a week before Christmas Day, adding new decorations each year, even some lights one year. After breakfast, Grandma Annie, Aunt Bertie and I sat around the tree to pass out presents. What stories that tree could tell!' Gordon paused to clear a catch in his throat.

'Eventually, we were too grown up for a Christmas tree. Aunt Bertie and I went to college. We weren't home for Christmas in this house for many years. Aunt Bertie and I didn't live here again when we had our own families and our own homes. You remember that Grandma Annie has visited us each year for Christmas. And we always had that big green, plastic Christmas tree.'

Gordon closed his eyes for a moment. He thought about Anne, Bertie and the tree; thoughts tinged with regrets for not fully appreciating those earlier Christmas Days around that special

Christmas tree. An image of his father pushed into those memories of long-ago Christmases. His throat tightened at these vivid images. A little voice broke his reverie.

'Dad, what happened to the tree?' asked Gordie, looking up into his father's dark eyes. Seeing his reflection in Gordie's eyes, Gordon stood up. He took Gordie's hand.

'Well, I don't know, son. Maybe it's still in the basement. Let's go look!'

Sue Colyer

My Working Life

"Come on, June, let's go."

How I wished later that I hadn't heard those words, especially in peak traffic at 5 o'clock in St. Georges Terrace.

When I was seventeen I used to consider myself lucky to have this red-haired round-faced gentleman pick me up in Great Eastern Highway early in the morning. I drove to work with him and he'd drop me off at the same place after work. At that time my salary was five pounds five shillings; my board was three pounds five shillings. Saving this money enabled me to save on fares, to buy the new clothes I badly needed. Over a year I was able to have some spare money for other necessities.

Mr. Rogerson was the Manager of the Claims Section at the S.G.I.O. He had a great sense of humour. On the way to work we'd tell each other the latest jokes and funny stories. These would lighten up our trip to Perth, especially on the days when the traffic was bumper to bumper.

At the end of a day's work, I would hear him call out down the corridor, "Are you ready? We're off!"

We walked out the front door of the S.G.I.O. heading for a side street on the other side of St. Georges Terrace where there was free parking. As we stood out on the footpath outside our building, and saw the traffic I remarked: "We'll never get across here."

"Yes we will, follow me," he instructed.

He reached the island in the middle of the road and as he looked back I saw the alarm in his eyes. He knew what was imminent. A motor bike came racing up the inside lane as I was crossing two rows of traffic. My recollection of the impact was very vague. I was unconscious. I remember waking up in a car on the way to Royal Perth Hospital. When I opened my eyes, Mr. Rogerson said "You've been in an accident," relating to me what had happened.

"Excuse me for laughing. It was so funny when the hoop of your petticoat was wrapped around the handle bars of the young man's bike."

I failed to see the funny side then, I could see my skirt was in tatters.

"By the way," he continued, "we found one of your shoes down the road; your foot stopped under the wheel of his bike. You'll have swelling and bruising there." Then he said, "I have to go home, I'll see you later."

After a thorough examination by a young doctor, his prognosis was: "Your injuries aren't too bad, it could have been worse."

"We'll keep you here for a couple of hours for observation, just in case you are concussed. You have a nasty lump on your head."

Just then a young man's face appeared at my bedside. "I'm the one who hit you on my motor bike," he confessed. "I'm sorry, but I thought the way was clear, I didn't expect anyone to be crossing the road there."

"That's okay," I assured him. "We'll cross at the lights next time."

"I hope you're alright," he said as he started to leave. "I'll check up on you later."

"Thanks," I said meekly.

He phoned back one hour later as I was due to be discharged. I assured him I was feeling better. I telephoned Patricia who had asked her father to come and drive me home. The nurses looked at my shredded skirt, laughing, "You can't possibly go home like that!" They proceeded to pin the sides and front of my skirt together. At that stage I didn't care.

On the way home I related the story about the accident. By now

I was able to see the funny side of it. Everyone laughed. When I got home I showed them the huge lump on the back of my head where I'd hit the road, my swollen ankle, all of the bruises on my body. I realized I had been lucky, only receiving minor injuries. I spent a few days at home recuperating on sick leave, feeling sore, but grateful I didn't have any broken limbs or permanent damage to my head. In retrospect, I'd had a lucky escape.

I contacted Elaine, my younger sister. She had previously been fostered by one of our mother's friends from Greenbushes. Elaine was too young to travel to Perth alone. The public transport buses to and from Beechboro on the weekends were few and far between. I visited her. This would entail spending the whole of Sunday travelling. It was worth it, believing as I did, we needed this contact and closeness. Elaine was able to talk to me about any little matter worrying her, which she did often.

As I was on a minimal wage I wasn't able to afford much besides the fares, just an occasional treat. Later on when my wages increased it was possible to help her in different ways. She asked for a push bike. "I need it to travel to and from the train station," she assured me. Elaine was now attending a girls' school which she found enjoyable, whereas previously she had felt intimidated and distracted by the boys in her class. She asked to move to another school, and was performing at a higher level. Elaine asked for help with books and uniforms. I assisted whenever I could afford it. Eventually she found the poultry farm too isolated, asking me, "Can you help to find me another place to stay after I finish school?" I said I would. When the time came, we made an application to the Community Welfare Department officer concerned with her welfare. Once this was approved Elaine was able to move to the same place where I was boarding in Victoria Park; she shared a room with me until I left for Melbourne six months later. Her foster parents were sorry to see her leave as they had grown attached to her. As she left, Elaine said, "Thank you for looking after me. I want to live with my sister now." Elaine was much happier when we were together.

One cold winter's day I arrived home from work to be greeted by my friend Patricia.

"I'm bored!" she declared. "Let's go to Melbourne for a working holiday for a year or so."

"But what if we can't find a job?" I questioned.

"I know we will," she assured me. "I'm a Receptionist, I can type. You've finished your stenography course and have had plenty of opportunity to practise your skills at your job at the S.G.I.O."

The idea sounded feasible. "We need a change," Patricia reminded me.

"Well, I'm a free agent," I said. "But you'll have to make your parents agree first. Why don't you talk to them, and then get back to me."

After more discussion, we decided to think about it for a week or two. A couple of weeks later when I arrived home from work, Trish was crying in her room; her mother had a look of thunder on her face. As I entered the lounge-room, this little old lady with a weathered face, horn-rimmed glasses, hair pulled back into a severe bun, charged at me. "I hope you didn't put her up to this!" she yelled.

"No, it was her idea," I answered quietly and calmly. "We are still thinking about it."

At that point Patricia came out of her room, eyes red from crying. She glared at her mother, saying: "We'll discuss it when you've calmed down." Her mother felt very threatened by this impending change, and spent the day sulking. Nothing more was said about the matter that day. A few days later as we all sat at the dinner table, Trish broached the subject of Melbourne once more. She assured me she had her father on her side. Bravely, Patricia announced: "I've enquired about the fares, compared the prices of flying, travelling to Melbourne by train and a berth on a cruise ship. Cost-wise, the last option was the best for us, meaning we could have a week's paid holiday on the way." I can still see the look of astonishment on her mother's weather-beaten face.

"Mum," her father intervened, "the girls are serious about this trip. I know you don't want to lose Patricia, but she'll always be our daughter. It's time to let her make her own decisions, she is nineteen now."

Silence followed.

I know this little old lady felt they had invested their future in this girl and now they were losing her. I had only been boarding at their house for a year and a half. I felt no closeness to them even though I admired and respected them. Trish's mother spent the next week refusing to talk to anyone, it seemed like an eternity. On the weekend when we came home from basketball, her mother broke the ice with, "Well, I've decided that you can go." Patricia said to me later, "That's a relief."

A few weeks later I ran into one of my friends from Parkerville, Beverley, who told me about the place where she was staying in East Victoria Park.

"There are two other girls living there you know," she said. "The couple who own this house welcome girls from children's homes. She advertises for them. I'll give you the telephone number. It's just like a real home here, we all feel accepted." This was six months before we left for Melbourne. She gave me the telephone number. I made arrangements to move in, asking Mr. and Mrs. Waddell, "Will it be alright if I stayed for six months? I will be leaving for Melbourne soon. Before I leave, I would like my younger sister to stay in my room until I return. If there is room for me when I come back, maybe we can both live here with you."

"Of course you can" Mrs. Waddell assured me.

There were arrangements to be made, clothes to buy, fares to be paid, people to tell.

"We're off on an adventure to Melbourne," we announced to all of our friends excitedly.

In a quiet moment with Patricia after work, I reminded her, "We'll all have to give notice soon." She agreed. Before our departure I announced to my boss in the Microfilm Department I would be leaving to go to Melbourne in a month's time.

"I thought you were happy here," she said.

As I looked into the eyes of this older lady I felt a sense of betrayal. For nearly three and a half years she had trained me, expecting me to take over her job as Head of the Microfilm Department. Miss Gavan Duffy was not healthy, having taken weeks off at a time. I knew that she was nearing retirement age.

"Wait until Mr. Wood, the Manager hears about this," she warned.

The following day I made an appointment to break the news.

"Good morning", he said as I entered the room with trepidation. "Sit down, June."

"I sat down quickly. "I don't know where to start," I said nervously.

"At the beginning will be fine."

"Two of my friends and I have decided to leave W.A. to travel to Melbourne and work for a year. We've been talking about it for some time. We've made plans to leave on a passenger ship next month. I'm giving plenty of notice so you can replace me."

As I looked into this man's clear blue eyes, I saw the disappointment.

"June, this is a very risky thing for you to do," he warned. "Especially as you have no parents to fall back on if anything goes wrong. Think carefully about this step."

After a long pause I replied. "I'm a qualified Stenographer; I've been taking care of myself for a long time. I know I will succeed."

"I know you will too," he smiled. He realised I had made up my mind. "We'll all be sorry to lose you. I'm going to write you a reference. It will help you find a job."

"Thank you," I muttered meekly. I escaped from his office, feeling like a traitor.

True to his word, he gave me a most commendable reference that opened doors for me later. I reminded myself I had learnt a lot at this place. I'd been very fortunate to work with so many supportive people for my first job. When I showed my friends my reference, especially Bernice from Parkerville, she laughed, "You should send a copy to that last Manager, rub his nose in it."

The next month passed by quickly. There seemed so much to do, so little time. Once our fares were paid, we started packing our clothes, saying our goodbyes. Trish had invited a new friend from work, Noelene, to accompany us. We agreed. Once we were on the ship we'd stay together, always take care of each other. If by any chance we became separated, we'd always get a message to the others informing them of our whereabouts. Patricia and I had been friends for a long time. We knew we could always trust each other. Patricia said: "I'm not too sure about Noelene. I don't know her that well but let's give her a chance." We hoped she would be a good friend.

As we farewelled our friends on the dock at Fremantle, we boarded a West/East passenger ship named the 'Kanimbla'. With tears in our eyes we waved frantically until the people standing on the wharf looked like little specks.

"Let's go down to our cabin."

June Cornock

Extract from A Scattering of Roses

Amsterdam Holiday:

A little something I wrote for friends heading to Amsterdam

Be careful Jean
don't go in there,
the Museum of Sex
people might stare.

Bob looks squeamish
he's really not sure
what you might
have in store.

Condoms and sex toys
gadgets galore,
mannequins in positions
you've never seen before.

'I'm not afraid
to try something new'
Jean says armed with her suitcase
shiny and blue.

'Don't be afraid Bob'
she gives him a wink.
'I'm off to the gift shop
to see what I think'.

'How can I help you?'
the salesman smiles.
'I'll take one of each
of those chocolate toys'.

'When I get home
there are friends that I know
that will love to enjoy
all I have to show'

Lucy Cotton

Diane

Written for a friend who had without realising it, booked on the same trip as me a few years ago

D is for
Diane who needed a break
a cruise might be nice
so she booked in one shake.

I is for
I want to
get away from it all
to meet new people, she thought
be they short, fat or tall.

A is for ambiance
peaceful surrounds
bobbing blue ocean
no kids on the sun deck lounge.

N is for
new faces and places to explore
distance ports and markets
she wants to see them all.

E is for
edgy when she discovers
that I'm on her cruise.
If she can't avoid me
she'll take to the booze

Lucy Cotton

Road Trip

Crows pick at the dead kangaroo by the roadside. It's 4 am and I'm on a road trip. Anna's been messaging a guy on Facebook and decided it was time they met.

'Come with me,' she'd begged. 'You might meet a cute guy.'

That was the last thing I wanted, but I needed a holiday. Staring at double yellow lines, the headlights on full beam, we leave Perth behind. Fishing rods clatter in the back.

'Remind me why we're taking fishing rods, and your smelly mutt?'

'Guys love chicks who fish. As for Charlie, he's my lucky charm,' Anna winks.

Sunrise appears in the rear vision mirror. Light dances across the ocean and I open the window to inhale the salty air. The soft morning breeze caresses my face and my grumpy mood dissolves. The dog whimpers.

'Charlie needs to pee,' said Anna. 'Let's take the turnoff to Hangover Bay.'

A wide expanse of sandy beach greets us. Leaping out of the car, Charlie sets off to explore. No sooner have our toes touched the sand and he's going ballistic barking in the dunes.

'I hope it's not a snake,' exclaims Anna.

The bobtail lizard bares its teeth egging Charlie on. Anna grabs him by his collar and hauls him back to the beach.

A white minivan ambles into the carpark and eight plump oldies clamour to the water's edge. Whoa! Our beach invaders strip off. With down-caste eyes, we get in the car. Like an accident scene where you know you shouldn't look, I do. Frolicking naked in the ocean, their German accents hang heavy in the air as we drive away.

A West Coast Eagles flag flutters in the breeze on the veranda of a weatherboard cottage. The communications tower overshadows the town, looming like a gatekeeper on watch. Pulling into the petrol station, off-road vehicles with bug-splattered windscreens and roo-bars dominate. A lone seagull eyes us suspiciously from the power lines as we indulge in toasted sandwiches.

Back on the road, Grey Nomads hauling caravans pass us in droves, heading south. Four hours into our trip and squatter shacks pop into view along the coast.

'Are we there yet?' I whine.

'Only a few more hours,' Anna reassures me.

Olive trees compete with wind-tortured gums on the outskirts of Geraldton.

'What's that smell?' I gag.

Anna glares in the rearview mirror at her dog.

Northampton servo is a hive of activity. I'm busting for the loo and dash inside for the key. Back outside, weary travellers at petrol pumps eye my prize, the dunny key. They know they'll have to wait. I mutter a humble prayer to the God of Toilets. *Please let it be clean and there be paper. Amen.*

Anna walks Charlie hoping he'll poop, and I offer to get lunch. The Bain Marie is a sea of brown; crumbed sausages, Chicko rolls, and pies. I order salad sandwiches.

'We don't have wholemeal luv.'

'Multigrain?'

'No Luv. Only white.'

Queued behind me, I can feel the truckie's eyes burning *bloody tourist*, into my back.

Anna glances at the sandwiches and choc milk I plonk on the

picnic table.

'Don't even ask,' I tell her.

We pass a large lake the colour of pink lemonade, dazzling in the sun. Ten million flies seize my face as I open the window, making me splutter. Anna thinks I'm hilarious.

Arriving at our destination, Kalbarri boasts three taverns, a chip shop, a bakery and a butcher's. Parking outside the pub, Anna disappears into the real estate agents for our key. A ute pulls up and a guy sporting a healthy mullet heads in the pub but not before throwing me a smile.

Our accommodation is clean and comfortable. Charlie approves of the backyard and immediately explores. I unload the car as Anna chats on her phone.

'I can't wait to meet you. See you at the pub and make sure your friend comes.'

Anna and What's His Name, are setting me up with one of his dopey mates. I hope it's not Mister Mullet. A recent breakup ended on a rather cold note, so men are off my *to do* list at the moment.

The cheesecloth dress complements her tan. Her only makeup, a hint of mascara. Anna's a tad dizzy, but she's a good friend.

'Are you wearing that?' She eyes my jeans and t-shirt.

'Hey, I'm not the one trying to impress. Besides, the world isn't ready for my white hairy legs.'

We farewell Charlie, sprawled out in the shade of the patio.

Pete guides us to a table in the beer garden.

'Greg's getting the drinks' he explains, giving me a wink. Pete and Anna look cosy gazing at each other holding hands. Then I see him. He makes his way past the blokes hanging about in the doorway. A couple of beers, a bottle of white wine tucked under his arm, and two glasses present no challenge. He oozes confidence. Not bad. Not bad at all.

'Nice to meet you. White wine?'

'Sure,' I manage.

The next few hours are all about him. I feign interest in his life, asking questions.

'I've been here five years. Pete was working up here, and I came for a visit and never left. I work for the Shire. Keep an eye on the town you might say.'

I'm only half-listening to him and enjoy exploring his sun-kissed face. Blue-grey eyes with sandy lashes and freckled nose. A strong jawline with salt and peppered light afternoon stubble becomes him.

'…so women don't get me, but I'm prepared to let you have a crack at trying to work me out.' He leans in close with a smirk on his face.

'Well, thank you, gentlemen, for a lovely afternoon. Anna, time we went home and checked on Charlie. He'll be desperate for a walk.' I stand up ready to leave. Anna and Pete's faces are aghast.

'Come back to my place for a while,' Pete begs Anna. I can tell she's keen. Greg looks like he couldn't give a toss. Anna chooses Pete over me.

'Fine. I'll walk the dog.' Storming back to the house I ignore the ocean demanding my attention. It dumps large waves on the shore. The gulls call *Kelly, Kelly*, to no avail.

Wine sloshes around in my head and stomach. Charlie's pleased to see me. I check the fridge for dog food and discover a bottle of white wine that seems to say, *well hello.*

The last of the afternoon light expires. Feeling a little woozy, I know I won't see Anna tonight. Falling into bed, I curse that damn man with his broad shoulders. Good thing I'm not interested.

My mouth feels dry. Sunlight glares through the window. I check to see if Anna's back. She isn't.

I head into town for breakfast. The aromas from the bakery permeate the air. Standing in line, two teenage boys in front of me can't decide what they want.

Bang, goes the door. An old broad with a sour face storms in and heads straight to the front of the queue. She grabs a bag of bread rolls, swinging them face-height like a hypnotist.

'How much?'

The woman behind the counter doesn't bat an eyelid. The old girl slaps a handful of coins down.

'Tourists!' She spits and bangs the door on the way out for good measure.

'Charlie.' He's not in the yard. The side gate flaps open in the morning breeze. The dry sandy street is empty. My heart races. Anna will kill me. After ten minutes of searching, I decide I need help.

The receptionist notes Charlie's description, promising to contact the ranger immediately. An hour later a van pulls up. I race outside, the path hot under my feet.

Charlie greets me like an old friend accompanied by a smiling Greg in khaki uniform.

'Thanks,' I mumble.

'Hold your horses' young lady. Your dog created havoc in Mrs Stanley's chook pen. I may have to press charges.'

Tears fill my eyes.

'I was only kidding. Let's go inside,' said Greg.

I wash my face and boil the kettle. We sip coffee and chat. He reassures me my tears are understandable.

'I've got to check out a cat issue in Port Gregory this afternoon. I wouldn't mind some company. You're not allergic to cats are you?'

'No, only men.'

He laughs, and we hear the front screen door bang.

'What's the ranger doing here? Greg, it's you.'

'You ok?' I ask.

'I'm wonderful,' says Anna. 'Pete's coming over later.'

Greg stands to leave. 'Pick you up at 1 pm?'

'It's a date,' slips out of my mouth.

Japanese tourists photograph the luminescent lake. The men in crisp white shirts and tailored pants, the women dressed to the nines.

'Crikey, they'll blend in with the locals in Port Gregory,' says Greg.

In the sleepy fishing hamlet, the weatherboard fishermen's shacks look deserted. Pulling into the caravan park it's hot and quiet. The only sound, flies buzzing around a bin.

The bell above the door jingles. A tanned blonde with a friendly face appears from out back.

'Hi Greg, thanks for coming.'

The cat crisis is over. The caravan park tenant got wind of Greg's visit, loaded her car, cats and all and was last seen heading north.

He suggests we have a swim. White sand crunches underfoot, my lily white legs a beacon for the sun. Salt water stings where I've dry-shaved in a hurry only an hour ago.

'It's freezing.'

Greg bounds into the ocean. I can't take my eyes off him.

'Don't go.' He stretches out a tanned arm as I rise from his bed. The ceramic tiles are cool underfoot and for a moment I ponder staying longer. I dress and give him a lingering goodbye kiss, agreeing to meet tomorrow.

I arrive home to find a red-eyed Anna with her arms around Charlie on the couch.

What's Pete done?'

'I asked him where to from here, and he said he wasn't looking for anything serious.' She sobs.

'You did use protection, right?'

She wails. I place a kiss on her forehead and tuck her into bed.

'You have a nap. I'll walk Charlie.'

There's a handful of fishermen on the beach. I see a guy sitting on an upturned bucket in front of his vehicle, rod in hand. It's Greg! Charlie bounds up to him.

I'm about to wave when she appears from the rear of the vehicle dressed in bikini and sarong. She's holding a baby. Greg looks at me, looks at her, and turns away.

Spinning on my heels, I power back to the carpark, calling Charlie without looking back. Bloody men.

The next morning our car crawls into Geraldton and we check into a caravan park. Anna doesn't want to be back on the road for a day or two. The doctor said she may feel some ill effects from the Morning-After Pill he prescribed.

Charlie and I walk to the lighthouse. Its steel tower stands proud and tall.

'What a shame I can't find a man as dependable as you,' I tell the lighthouse.

I have missed calls from Greg. Steeling myself, I phone him. He apologises for any misunderstanding and begs to see me. Clutching the phone tighter I hear him explain,

'She's my sister.'

What have I done?

'I'm on my way,' he says. 'Stay right where you are. Promise you'll wait for me?'

'I promise.'

Lucy Cotton

Holiday in Israel

My husband Martin and I picked a rather dangerous time, May 1967, for a holiday of a lifetime in Israel. We left our two children, a girl aged six and boy aged eight years, with my husband's parents. We knew trouble was brewing in Israel but wasn't that always the case! We arranged to stay in a hotel in Natanya, a seaside resort not far from Tel Aviv. Martin's sister Ruby, who lived in Haifa had booked to stay at our hotel as she thought we needed a native to show us around.

The name of our hotel, 'Ofakim', was unfortunate because it caused us acute embarrassment. Israel is a small country about the size of Wales, so inevitably we bumped into people from the U.K. When they enquired where we were staying, we tried nonchalantly to pronounce the name of our hotel, but they would laugh loudly and shout out 'O fuk im!' Their reactions reflected how we actually felt about the hotel because while we were unpacking we opened the wardrobe and were confronted by a couple of enormous cockroaches. It fazed my husband because the creatures took second place only to spiders in his scale of abhorrence. It was war on his part, an act of bravery, when he attacked them with a broom and sprayed them to saturation point with aerosol.

The cuisine was basic, they served cornflakes, cold, soft boiled eggs, and burnt toast for breakfast. The staff had little idea of customer service, and they rarely made an appearance in the morning. They spoke only Hebrew, while we only knew two words of their language, *Ken* meaning Yes and *Lo* for No. When we learned the word jam was *Riba*, we managed, after much gesticulation, to get them to substitute it for marmalade. Ruby told us that young Israelis were called *Sabras* which means prickly pears. She said that the young generation was brought up not to kowtow to anyone, so we had no choice but to put up with their abysmal service.

We left the hotel and decided to explore our surroundings. We fell in love with Natanya, as we breathed in the aroma of Frangipani and other exotic plants. People who thronged the streets were mostly Jews of European countries, some were auburn-haired and others blond like my husband, but there were also darker-skinned Jews of Middle Eastern origin who had been expelled from the surrounding countries. The cafes were filled with diners, and others bought falafel from the street stalls. For us it was a contrast to England where we mostly stayed indoors because of the cold miserable climate. We dined at a cafe and realised we should accustom ourselves to Middle-Eastern food and soon preferred it to the bland food which at that time was served in England.

Much of the time we travelled by bus. Bus drivers were considered the elite because they belonged to a strong Union, and were well paid. In Israel, it was said that there were more doctors than dockers because the country was saturated with migrant professional people, while artisans were at a premium. We travelled to Tel Aviv and were surprised at the many tall buildings because it was less than twenty years since the state of Israel had been founded. We took the lift to the top of the tallest building at that time 'The Shalom Tower'. A crowd had gathered and we were told that a Brit (circumcision) was about to take place. We wondered if they chose the venue as a symbol of male virility? My husband, with his video camera, made his way to the front where the crowd parted thinking he was the official photographer. The baby lay on a table, the mohel who was a rabbi and trained doctor, opened the nappy and almost with a sleight of hand which lasted less than a minute, the deed was done. The baby who gave a piercing scream was given wine to suck on the rabbi's sterile finger then handed to his mother where he commenced to suckle.

Martin's cousin Dorothy, together with her husband Frank, had been amongst the founders of Kibbutz Amiad close to the sea of Galilee. Against their parents' wishes they had eloped before going to university. At first the Kibbutz farmed produce and were self-supporting, but by now they had industries and supplied reticulation to Australia. The practice of children sleeping in dormitories had been abandoned in favour of sleeping in their parents' houses. The children were fiercely independent and had the run of the Kibbutz. We stayed overnight and had communal breakfast at eight, a late start as some of the members had already put in two hour's labour on the farm. Many non-Jewish university students visited the Kibbutz for the fruit picking season. Initially it had been an idyllic Communist-like venture, but many of the young people had left the Kibbutz favouring materialism.

We took a trip to Safed, which is high on the hill close to the Syrian and Lebanese border. It is an artistic and spiritual colony where they study the Kabbalah (mystical Hebrew book). Wherever we went we were surrounded by enemies whose sole object was to destroy Israel. But on an optimistic note we visited a Druze village, where friendly Palestinians who had all the advantages of health and education lived in harmony side by side with the Israelis.

When we visited Nazareth, an Arab guide, who boasted he could speak six languages, gave us an unintelligible commentary supposedly in English. He kept saying 'Jesus in a flash', but we were enlightened by another tourist who said he means 'Jesus in the flesh.' This Polish tourist said 'T anahis guide speaks all languages with the same expertise as he speaks English.' On another occasion we floated in the Dead Sea where it was so buoyant, because of the salt, we could neither sink nor swim.

In the Negev, we climbed up to Masada where zealots committed suicide rather than surrender to invaders. When we strolled around Jerusalem we were told to wear modest clothes when we passed through Mia Sherim, which is the Orthodox Religious section. We felt compelled to visit Yad Vashem where they house the testaments of those who had experienced the Shoah (Holocaust). We were traumatised because 'man's inhumanity to man' was beyond comprehension. Young Israelis didn't want to dwell on that horrific time when Jews went like 'lambs to slaughter.' Their motto was 'Never Again', and the civilians, both men, and women, who had trained for compulsory military service were ready to fight when the situation arose. If they didn't help themselves it was unlikely that others would come to their aid.

Our mood lightened when the festivities for the Anniversary of the Day of Independence took place throughout the country. Young and old were dancing in the streets dressed in blue and white, the colour of the Israeli flag; we shared the pride of the people's many achievements. When the young pioneers came to the country it is true there were Arabs farming orange groves and making a meagre living off the land, but there were also swamps ridden with mosquitoes and much barren land. The idealistic youths on the Kibbutz worked selflessly; it has been said 'they made the desert bloom.' At the United Nations the majority of nations voted in favour of the biblical right of Jews, a dispersed people, to reclaim their country after suffering so much persecution which culminated in 'The Holocaust.' Most Zionists in Israel are not observant Jews, but they feel strongly about the necessity to have independence, and protection from the scourge of anti-Semitism. Many Jews who live in other democratic countries such as Australia are loyal to their adopted country, but they regard Israel as their safety net. For this reason they support it both morally and financially.

We sat in a cafe one evening drinking coffee and eating our favourite cake Cream Schnitz, layers of flaky pastry filled with vanilla cream. We were amazed when trucks loaded with soldiers drove by. Ruby told us war was imminent, that Nasser had blocked the Straits of Tiran, and the countries surrounding Israel were planning to invade. She hadn't told us before because she wanted us to enjoy our holiday. We couldn't understand the Hebrew news, so we had behaved like 'Innocents abroad.'

The following day was when we had previously planned to leave; in fact the Israelis were anxious for all tourists to leave before war broke out. A car came for us in the morning, all traffic had been mobilised, and we drove past soldiers in camouflaged uniforms. We arrived at Lod airport where chaos reigned. We felt guilty we were leaving while other volunteers were flying in to help, but we had to return to our family. Eventually we boarded our VC10 and were relieved when it took off because it was rumoured the airport might be targeted.

A couple of days later, when we were home, The Six Day War broke out, Israel had made a pre-emptive attack on their enemies. At this time most of the Western Countries supported them. They conquered much of the Negev and Gaza, which provided a distance between them and their aggressors. Later they gave back Gaza only for it to be taken over by Hamas, a terrorist .organisation. How sad that this conflict has not been peacefully resolved.

Our young children were happy to see us. They had been too young to realise the danger – as if it were a movie, they thought it was an exciting situation. We didn't disillusion them.

Pat Curtis

Christmas in Luanshya

Christmas was only days away when, in 1950, we arrived in the mining town of Luanshya, in the country now known as Zambia.

My father had worked for Lake View and Star gold mine in Kalgoorlie. My mother hated living there – too hot, too dry, too dusty, and too lonely. One day my father came home from work with the question: How would you like to go and live in Northern Rhodesia. Her reply was: Yes please. Where is it?

Once he accepted the offered position, my father's presence was required immediately and he took the quick route - seaplane which island-hopped across the Indian Ocean, arriving in Cairo at the beginning of the Suez crisis. He and his fellow-travellers were promptly arrested as British spies and kept on a houseboat for four days before the Egyptians decided to allow them to continue their grasshopper run through Africa to their destination. The journey took them two weeks.

My mother was left to clear up the house in Kalgoorlie, store the furniture, and find a means to get us to central Africa, and accommodation in Perth until our ship, the *SS Gothic*, sailed for Cape Town. From there, it was coal-fueled train through the heat and dust of southern Africa to Ndola, railway town for the three mines (later, five), collectively known as the Copperbelt. The journey took about five days, some of it without water because the whiskey-imbibers drank it all, through desert, grassland, and dense bush, past alien villages with even more alien faces. In those days, Ndola was a dusty little dot of a place, and her heart must have sunk at the sight of it. There followed twenty miles in pitch dark, on dirt road through thick African bush.

We arrived in Luanshya late at night and were taken to the house that my father had shared with another man until our arrival. A bachelor pad. Company furniture, ancient beds with mosquito nets, a one-burner stove, no laundry. I think my mother determined to get herself back home at the earliest opportunity. To the endless delight of her two younger daughters, the bathroom had an internal lavatory with a pull-chain for flushing.

Her feelings changed next morning when a lady named Bett Hamilton arrived with daughter Isla in tow. Wife of the Personnel Manager, Scottish, organiser-extraordinaire, she carted us off on a sight-seeing tour. Luanshya, the garden town of the Copperbelt, presented itself in glorious tropical colour at that time of year: the jacarandas spreading a carpet of purple as the canopy released the blossom; poinsettias and African flame trees acknowledged Christmas with their vibrant red display; pink hibiscus and magenta bougainvillea hedges lined the streets; and mango and loquat trees produced fruit available to everybody. After Kalgoorlie, my mother was hooked.

Bett took us to a morning tea party, to be welcomed by a friendly group of women from all parts of the world, and their children. I remember my first sight of Isla, two years older than I, in a red tartan dress with gathered skirt, frills at the shoulders and, at the end of her long pigtail, the biggest ribbon I'd ever seen. My mother must have admired her too because I remember having many such dresses and ribbons.

Isla's cat produced kittens on Christmas Eve, five of them she named Holly, Ivy, Mistletoe, Santa, and Nicholas. The promise that I could have Nicky was my first Christmas present in Africa.

My mother had arranged for the packing cases to precede us, but of course, none had arrived, and we had only the clothes we'd brought with us. My parents were told not to bring furniture because almost anything we wanted would be available. Not in the shops, though. People came and went or were transferred between the towns on the Copperbelt like birds change nests, and rather than go to the expense of moving, they sold their furniture and bought another lot in the next town. Auction sales were an almost nightly occurrence and social event. 'Are you going to the auction at 21C tonight? The Joneses are going back to England and they have some lovely local wood furniture.' Thus we acquired lounge and dining suites, rattan chairs for the verandah, occasional tables, curtains, cushions, ornaments and ashtrays, crockery and cutlery, none of it new but most with a uniquely African touch. In the meantime we would manage with what was already in the house.

We had three servants who, with our limited knowledge of Australian Aborigines, terrified us until we were used to them. There was a garden boy whose face and name changed weekly since the occupation of gardener was generally regarded as a restful one, and each, in turn, was found asleep under a tree. Jappie, the houseboy, was technically the boss man of the house, although there was some dispute about this with Cookie whose domain was the kitchen. My mother readily became accustomed to having servants and took to the social life with the others. She had much to learn!

That first Christmas, Jappie surprised us with a table exquisitely laid with glassware and silver, items we didn't own and were certainly not in the house. He had done a whip around of the other servants in the neighbourhood, to set a proper table for his new family.

Jappie was a character who, even after nearly fifty years and a multitude of servants, my sisters and I remember with affection. After Christmas lunch was cleared, Jappie would don a white tropical suit and gloves and Panama hat, and, with malucca cane in hand, would go to visit the ladies. At first he walked; later, with the help of a loan from my father, he acquired a bicycle. 'I am a Boy,' he explained, 'I need a bicycle.'

Whether his mind was on the ladies or his imagination extended no further than the next ten seconds, we'll never know, but coming home from work one day, my father witnessed Jappie directing his front wheel at a wooden plank on the road through which stuck a line of nails. Along it he sailed as if riding a tight-rope, and both tyres popped. There was much sadness when my father refused to provide two new tubes, and Jappie had to do without his bicycle until he'd saved the money.

A certain animosity existed between Jappie and Cookie, possibly tribal, probably because of Jappie's free and easy lifestyle. One Christmas Eve my parents were at an official function - there were always important visitors to the mine - when one of the waiters sidled up to my mother and said: 'Dona, your cook is here; he wants to see you.' This was such an unusual occurrence my mother thought the house must be on fire or some such. She hurried to the back gate and there was Cookie with kitchen cleaver in hand.

'That Jappie,' he said, 'he steals my woman last night. I am going to kill him but first I am telling you, Dona, so you are finding another boy to do your work while I am in the Little House of King Georgie.' (their expression for gaol) My mother sorted it out: Jappie escaped the panga and Cookie lived on.

One of the best things about Christmas in Luanshya was the decorations. Our house had streamers made from strips of crinkle paper, fastened to a string tied to a central light, twirled and strung around the room, creating a multi-coloured canopy effect. In a later house, the front enclosed verandah, what we would now call a family room, had two white spherical light fittings on which my mother drew Father Christmas faces, and attached beards. To Nicky, our cat, these were alien beings that must be driven off, and he would spend much of his time taking swipes at them, darting from chair to chair and climbing on anything that would bring him nearer to them.

Every year we had a Christmas tree, a big one, a real one, the branch of a pine tree brought from a plantation somewhere. In that heat, the tree barely lasted through Christmas and had deposited most of its needles on the floor by 6th January. When they were old enough, my sisters and their boyfriends took over decorating the tree, and it became an occasion from which my parents and I were banned until the doors were thrown open and we were allowed in to oo and ah. One Christmas one of the boyfriends donned my sister's pink fairy costume and a pair of swimming flippers and laboriously performed what thereafter became *The Frog Dance*

Most people had a tree, and it was one of our Christmas treats to load the back of my father's work ute with kids and he would drive all around town so we could admire the trees in people's front windows, and their outside decorations.

There were many parties at that time of year. I always had a Christmas party, as did many of my friends. Planning had to be done early or there would be no day available on which to have your party. As well as these, the various departments on mine and in town had their own children's parties. Father Christmas would arrive at each in a variety of ways: a decorated float, a fire engine, a parachute, whatever the department and Father Christmas had access to. There were also adult parties, with some adults regularly causing all kinds of harmless mayhem, and dances on Christmas and New Year's Eve. I was too young for these, but I remember my mother spending hours sewing sequins and beads on fairy princess-type ballgowns for my sisters.

On Christmas Day everybody held open house and there was much to-ing and fro-ing and merry jingle bells everywhere. Opposite us lived a family my mother was never too keen on my visiting, and finally banned me from going there. To this day I don't know why. The middle child was a girl I was desperate to be friends with, probably because of the mystery surrounding the family. From her I learned that mother had departed, never to return. Father, an underground miner, kept things going, sometimes loudly, and with vehemence. There was an older brother of whom I have no recollection and a younger brother named Alec who was hell on wheels. If ever a louder than usual noise occurred, there would be a brief silence and then father's voice would roar out "That's you, Alec," followed by bellows and wails of protestation from Alec. I remember one Guy Fawkes night … Another time, another story.

Christmas in Luanshya was friends and food, lights and colour, people and noise, and the spirit of giving beamed so brightly it filled everybody with gladness and goodwill.

Pat Fletcher

Will the Real Santa Stay Put

'Twas the day before Christmas and all of the shops
Had turned up the pressure, pulled out the stops

A fake Santa Claus wiggled his hips
Sang Jingle Bells without moving his lips.

The kiddies slid past peering in fear
To the real Father Christmas, sitting quite near.

One at a time they sat on his knee
Whispered a wish, took a toff-ee.

One little girl, a proper young miss
Threw her arms round his neck and planted a kiss.

'Santa,' she said, 'you're the main man –
Please will you bring me a doll and a pram.'

Then the Santa cops pitched, their faces quite pale
'Come Santa,' they said, 'you're off to gaol.'

The children cried loudly, mums gave a bellow
'Don't take away Santa: he's a jolly good fellow.

'It's the perverts and wowsers who need to be taught
To raise their sick minds to more uplifting thought

'So the kids of the future can all have the joy
'Of asking a *real* Santa for one special toy.'

Pat Fletcher

In 2005 it was deemed inappropriate that children sit on Santa's knee, and the practice was banned.

Travel Hiccups

It took months to organise. Friends had mixed opinions about it – some pronounced me brave and their gaze was envious; others said I was mad, but their contemptuous expressions hid their fear of doing the same. When it came to the point I have to confess I agreed with them all.

As Barry turned his back to plod towards the exit, having deposited me and my bags at check-in, I had a hard job resisting the urge to race after him. The infatuation of a new relationship demanded I stay – how could I think of leaving him for three and a half months? What if things went wrong?

Through my mind flashed the places I'd yearned to see, the people I'd arranged to visit, coach tours, train rides, a cruise, helicopter over Grand Canyon, north to Alaska. And of course, there was all that money, wasted if I didn't board that plane.

I'd sworn never again to be held back by a man, no matter what the circumstances. I grabbed my cases and marched to the check-in. My dream was about to become reality; I'd planned it precisely; nothing could go wrong.

The first crisis hit me on my arrival at Los Angeles airport. Getting there had been lengthy and tiring, but uneventful, even quite pleasant. My flight companion was a pilot with North West Airlines, who entertained me with tales of his fishing and camping trips with mates to Kodiak Island in Alaska, where all food must be secured in metal boxes with bear-proof locks. One night, someone forgot to lock the box and a bear clawed an entry into their tent. They escaped unhurt but had to wait three days for the helicopter to come and get them.

I'd lived in Africa but where I was heading sounded rougher than anything I'd experienced.

The pilot strode off with his mates once we were outside Customs and Immigration, and I confidently surveyed the drivers with placards bearing names of passengers to be collected. I'd pre-paid for a limousine to take me to Anaheim where I was to join my first tour group.

No placard with my name on it. I waited until all those meeting Qantas from Sydney had left, and resisted the urge to take the next flight home. Thirty-six hours into my dream holiday and I was stuck at an airport in a strange city in an unfamiliar country where I knew no one. Was this an omen?

No, merely the first challenge. Stop being a defeatist, I told myself. Find a phone and ring the limo company. Second challenge: no US dollars and an incomprehensible telephone system. Up an escalator and through a couple of halls, brought me to the Information desk. They weren't particularly interested but phoned the number on my voucher. The limo company had no idea where my driver might be – they were based in New York. Several more phone calls and numerous radio calls to local drivers seemed to indicate that mine had become lost, mislaid or otherwise occupied. I had begun to wonder if I'd have to find alternative transport to Anaheim, two hours away, or give up and go home when another driver from the same company pitched up. He'd heard the radio calls and, taking pity on me, returned to take me under his wing. He'd met another passenger, a lady who'd been on my plane and who was joining the same tour group. It beats me why they needed two limousines to take two little old ladies to the same destination. Maybe they realised they didn't but neglected to tell me.

Crises No. 2 was even more unnerving. Having been awestruck by Grand Canyon, Yosemite, the Boulder Dam complex and Las Vegas, we looked forward to our last excursion on that Californian tour - Alcatraz. We were dropped at Fisherman's Wharf, early enough to look around and have lunch. After that, our instructions were to be at a certain gate at a certain time to collect our tickets and board the ferry.

First, the loo. This turned out to be a large metal box something like our street electrical junction boxes, but red. Self-cleaning and antiseptic, they are coin-operated and so well sealed that, but for the line of people waiting, we'd probably have passed it by without realising.

I viewed this contraption with deep mistrust. Anything sealed against the outside world holds the potential to trap me forever. However, others were emerging unscathed, and I was desperate. When my turn came, I took coins from wallet, inserted them into the slot and, with pounding heart, stepped into the solid steel trap, barely controlling my urge to scream as the door slid shut.

Inside was a pleasant surprise: gleaming stainless steel and everything automatic including the flush mechanism and the taps. But no time to marvel – get on with it and get out as quickly as possible.

About half an hour later, I unzipped my handbag to check wallet for tickets. No wallet!

When I travel, the rule is: a place for everything, and if you take it out put it back. In my panic, I must have broken the rule and put the wallet down when I went to the loo.

By this time the red shed had accommodated a number of other people, swilling itself each time, and the chance of my money and various cards still being there was probably nil. Still, I had to make sure.

I managed to persuade the person next in line to allow me to check (first borrowing the necessary coins so I could get in), but, as I expected, it wasn't there.

I rejoined my group, furious that I'd miss the tour of Alcatraz, and at the same time trying to control my terror. I put hand in jacket pocket to haul out hankie to wipe away tears and encountered – my wallet. The trip could proceed.

My first evening in Vancouver threw up the third crisis. After an amazing tour through Alaska during which the highly efficient and solicitous tour company had escorted, cajoled and sometimes nursed us from Anchorage, by Midnight Sun Express through Denali National Park, to Fairbanks; from there ten hours by coach across largely uninhabited vastness – kind of like travelling through Western Australia – to Whitehorse, and on to Skagway where we boarded the Regal Princess for a 4-day cruise to Vancouver.

I'd organised to spend ten days on my own, so as to explore a city I'd heard so much about. Tours are educational and keep you safe, but there is never enough time to sit and absorb or return for another look.

The first two nights were covered by an hotel package, enough time to find further accommodation and to work out a sight-seeing plan. I'd heard that B&Bs in Vancouver were first class, run by friendly people who delighted in directing visitors around their beautiful city. I'd gained a lot of confidence since that arrival in Los Angeles and felt perfectly confident that all would go smoothly.

By 8.30 am I'd disembarked, and found a taxi which took me to my hotel. Check-in was 2 pm. The receptionist suggested I leave my luggage in the back room and take a ferry to explore the markets on Granville Island. The terminal was just over the road, across a big empty carpark (it was Sunday), down a pathway which went left, then … I lost track but found my way with no trouble.

Back at the hotel at about 3 pm, I checked into my 11th floor big, lovely corner room with huge windows and wonderful view. I shed handbag, camera, backpack and shrugged off my jacket. Feeling a bit lost and lonely after having had constant company for the previous twelve days, I decided to kill some time before dinner with a bath or a nap. Either way, more clothes had to come off, and I had just removed my top when the hotel alarm sounded.

These things happen: I wasn't very concerned. Probably an accident or maybe a test? The likelihood of there being a real fire the moment I turned up was not very great. On the other hand … since it was a Sunday… perhaps they thought it was a good day to have a fire drill. I began to re-load my body with travelling gear. The alarm stopped. Oh! A mistake!

No, it wasn't! No sooner had I removed everything once more, than off it went again, and this time it pealed on and on.

Voices in the passage outside my door told me others were milling around, wondering. I'd read the Emergency directions (another rule about travelling), grabbed handbag and door key, left the rest, and went out to join them. A man, his wife, and two children, and an elderly couple were as nonplussed as I was. We agreed to find the stairs and get ourselves down to reception. Down we trudged, in dim light, encountering others from each of the other ten floors, all quite nervous, sniffing for smoke. Finally, we emerged into the foyer, anxious and blinking against the bright light.

It was about half an hour before we could extract any information, but yes, it was real: smoke in the basement laundry; the fire brigade was on its way. They took their time while all guests milled around the lobby wondering if we were about to be burned to death or if it was a hoax after all. Two hours went by before we were allowed back upstairs. By that time I was thoroughly unnerved, had had enough of Canada, of travelling and had lost all interest in catching up with friends. I wanted to go home.

But a good night's sleep cures most miseries, and a long day on high alert most of the time ensured that I slept well in spite of the fear of more fire alarms.

The fourth and final crisis was more a test of strength and fortitude than potential disaster, and perhaps by then I was well used to finding my way and coping with the unexpected.

British Rail, and my train from Guildford in England to Dorchester was not so efficient. I'd explored the Rockies by coach, stayed in several hotels without mishap, travelled by train across Canada to Toronto, taken two flights via Chicago to Washington DC, and British Airways to London, spent several days with a friend in Haslemere, Surrey. The next stage was a direct train to Dorset.

Except that somewhere along the way, British Rail decided this train would go no further. We had five minutes to disembark, march to the end of the platform, climb steps to cross the tracks, down another flight on the other side, and leap onto the waiting train. No porters. No trolleys of any kind. My case now bulged considerably more than it had done, as did the heavy backpack and I carried several other items. I wondered how British Rail would handle a visiting heart attack on one of their unmanned rural stations. But I was grateful not to be lugging a 4m. surfboard as well, like the two young men in my section of the train.

In travel as in life, no matter how much wonder and excitement you encounter, crises punctuate the enjoyment. Perhaps they play as important a role as the pleasure, separating the spectacular and amazing by unforgettable dramas.

Pat Fletcher

Holiday Impressions

Endless patchwork of colours
greens, browns, vivid yellows
paddocks of dandelions
crops of wheat
fields of fallow.
The emu, the mallee hen
the fox and the crow
kangaroos bound, bulls bellow
flash of a parrot's rainbow wings
high above a magpie sings
sheltering in eucalypti tall
the cockatoos voice their raucous call
shaggy rams drink from dams
ewes cosset newborn lambs
children's laughter
a pup at play
the bark of the dogs
with a fox at bay.
Clusters of everlasting flowers
freshening winds, silver showers
cotton-wool clouds scudding low
gurgling streams gush and flow.

When day dies ghost owls fly
across a wide cobalt sky
silvery-white bobs a rabbit's tail
as it scuttles past on a moonlit trail.
Doves, willy-wag-tails, swallows bring
holiday cheer to a flowering spring.

Robin Giraudo

Holiday Lament

Why, why, why did I say yes? Travelling and sight-seeing are not my forte. I'm much happier in my own back yard, so why in a moment of insanity did I agree?

Last week, surprise, surprise, husband Harry, who never wants to leave his home town much less the country, came puffing into the kitchen and announced: "Jerry and Trudy are off to Singapore. He wants you to come to keep Trudy company."

"Singapore with Jerry Jerome and his anaemic wife? You've got to be joking!"

"C'mon Pammy, it's a five-star hotel. None of that cooking and cleaning you're always bitching about. You'll love it."

Cajoling, coupled with abuse eventually won me over, though I must admit the lure of luxury finally seduced me: I imagined floating in a pristine pool, daily massages, maids to make the beds, and chocolates on the pillow. Laundry collected and returned ironed to perfection. A tired housewife's Shangri-La. Singapore here I come!

Aeroplanes aren't my favourite mode of transport, and to make an anxious flight unbearable, Jerome had booked the smoking section. The trio, as I'd dubbed Jerome, Harry, and Trudy, chain-smoked their way to our destination. By the time we arrived in Singapore my sinuses burned like a furnace.

Customs proved mighty unpleasant. I struck a trumped-up officious little fellow, I immediately labelled 'misogynist.' When he found my tablets in the bowels of my suitcase he exclaimed, "Why are you hiding your pills?"

"I'm not hiding anything," I protested, and muttered under my breath, "Moron."

"So many. Why you have so many pills?"

"They're pills everyone takes on a trip if they've got any sense. Pills for vomiting and diarrhoea, which I believe are rampant in your country. Pills for indigestion, constipation, and anxiety and I'm sure as hell suffering from a dose of that now." *Next thing the little bastard will be wanting to strip search me,* I thought in panic and rummaged frantically in my handbag for prescriptions. I thrust them at him and after painstakingly examining each one he reluctantly let me go.

Outside the airport, we waited half an hour for pick up, and an uneasy feeling tugged at my solar plexus as we boarded the empty vehicle. It didn't strike me as being a five-star hotel sort of bus. Every time we approached a brightly lit, posh building with a fountain, my spirits lifted, and sank again as we chugged past. Eventually we pulled up at a poorly lit five-storey building, which I found out later was on the edge of Chinatown. No garden or fountain, not even a birdbath. Stark realisation hit me. I'd been conned.

We clanked our way to the fifth floor in an ancient lift. The accommodation wouldn't have rated two stars much less five: An old-fashioned double bed, covered with a faded bedspread, took pride of place in the middle of our dingy room. A stain of moisture, complements of the leaking air-conditioner, tracked its way across the muddy-coloured carpet. Lank, lace curtains partly obscured the magnificent view of a filthy brick wall.

Dazed with disappointment, I accompanied the delightful trio to our first meal in Singapore. Jerome, true to his stingy nature, took us to a cheap eating joint. The cook sported a bespattered apron and a grubby chef's hat. A pink fluid circulating in a glass container on the counter spelt instant typhoid and I wondered, *Will I escape Singapore alive?*

Jerome ordered Mapasures, thin pancakes filled with onions, egg, and various unknown ingredients. I reassured myself the hot food would destroy any gut-devouring bacteria. Who knows if our sinister Chef hadn't thrown a dog or two into the pot?

Later that night, lying on a lumpy mattress, listening to the drip, drip, drip of the leaking air-conditioner that cranked into life every half hour, I wept silent, enraged tears. Harry snored the night away in a drunken stupor, oblivious to his dismal surroundings. I restrained myself from shoving a handful of sheet into his gaping mouth.

Jerome, bearable in small doses, on a daily basis proved intolerable. His main occupations were eating and shopping, and he expected everyone to go along with him. Inevitably he stretched the elastic of my tolerance to breaking point and a confrontation occurred. One lunchtime, without consulting anyone else, he ordered a plethora of dishes.

"How are we going to eat all this?" My words came out in an exasperated squawk. "Do you think we're made of money to waste on unnecessary food?"

"We'll eat it, don't you worry your little head about that."

"More than your fair share, you can bet your life on that, you great glutton."

Harry butted in. "Fair go, Pammy, don't be so bloody aggressive. Give poor Jerry a go."

I shoved back my chair nearly toppling it to the floor. "And you, you money-spending maniac can fuck off too. You and your lying fat friend can go to hell." I stormed out and somehow found my way to the hotel. If anyone had accosted me, I'd have torn them to shreds. Angry as a sackful of weasels, I locked the bedroom door with a grunt of satisfaction. Harry and his snores could spend the night with his obnoxious mates.

The next day Jerome, Harry, and Trudy caught a train to Kuala Lumpur. Sulkily I refused to go. I'd lost all faith in Jerome and Harry, and Trudy proved dismal company. Fifteen years younger than her husband, she followed him around like a puppy dog, playing the role of little girl to big daddy.

After I'd bid them a surly goodbye I accosted the hotel manager, and for a small fee, he found me a more suitable room. Then I picked up the phone and ordered a massage.

"How long you stay in Singapore?" the masseuse asked as she stroked, rubbed and pummelled.

"Ten days."

"Very long time. Usually only four days people stay in Singapore. They shop and go home."

"I've shopped myself silly and to tell you the truth I'm ready to go home this minute."

"Are you here by yourself?"

"No. My friends are visiting Kuala Lumpur for a couple of days."

"Why Kuala Lumpur? Just another city. They should have gone Penang, much nicer."

"When they return I'm looking forward to visiting the Tiger Balm Gardens."

"Tiger Balm Gardens gruesome, not for nice lady like you."

I wouldn't have minded visiting Penang. As for the Tiger Balm Gardens, I later regretted not heeding her advice.

Two days later the trio arrived back in Singapore, Trudy beside herself, crying, vomiting, and shitting. "It was ghastly," she told me. "You're so lucky you didn't come, it's dirty and stinking. We stayed at this horrible place where the guests partied all night and Jerry and Harry got drunk, and I felt like I was dying and no-one cared."

"Possibly a touch of the dog," I ventured.

"Could've been anything. They served us steaks but it didn't look like beef. We came back on the bus. It was cheaper and Jerry had spent lots of money on food and drink. The Malaysian bus drivers are reckless, crazy men. After a couple of close calls I closed my eyes and hung onto Jerry for the rest of the trip."

Yeah, big hero Jerry with the cast-iron guts, I thought. *The alcohol probably killed any germs those two boozers ingested.* I rummaged around in my emergency medicine bag and gave her some pills to tide her over till she could see a doctor. I doubt her caring husband took her, probably too stingy to pay the bill, but later events would prove more expensive than a doctor's visit.

The next day Harry, Jerome and I left Trudy behind in close vicinity to the toilet and visited the Tiger Balm Gardens. Bizarre is the only word to describe the place. What remained in my mind was the punishments depicted in the Ten Courts of Hell, a deterrent no doubt to wickedness. We gazed on statues and dioramas of unfortunate victims with bloody necks minus heads, people skewered, crushed and disembowelled. The horrendous images haunted my dreams for the rest of what I can only describe as a thoroughly disappointing holiday.

Ten days of Jerome's Singapore, rabbit warrens, smog, endless shopping, traffic, pollution, aching feet, thunderous sinuses and sleepless nights finally came to an end. At last we were at the airport headed for home. Entering its doors, I danced a jig.

"Cut it out Pammy, you're making a fool of yourself," Harry remonstrated.

Trudy was nowhere to be seen. "Better go check the ladies," Jerome ordered me. "She's never been right since the K.L. trip."

I heard her throwing up as I opened the door. A voice crashed over the intercom, "Flight 64 to Sydney, Australia leaves in 30 minutes. Please prepare to board the aircraft."

"How are you going in there, Trudy?" I felt a panic attack coming on and tried not to shout. She came out pale and bedraggled. "Splash your face with cold water," I urged her, "it'll make you feel better." I pushed her towards the basin. "And try to hurry it up. It's time to go."

On our way out we met Jerome and Harry headed in the opposite direction. "We're going to change our money," Jerome explained.

The devious prick wants to miss the plane, I thought, *and have an excuse for more days off work. More days eating and shopping in Singapore.*

"Too late for that, we need to board the plane."

"Plenty of time, not to worry, relax old girl."

The pressure in my head mounted, the pounding in my ears thundered, "Go ahead, change your bloody money you scheming fat bastard. I'm boarding with or without you." I left the trio staring after me as I galloped towards the check-in counter.

After the debilitating passive smoking episode on the way over I'd made it my business to change my return seat to a non-smoking section, so didn't know whether the trio had boarded until we touched down in Sydney.

As I walked across the tarmac I saw two gowned and masked men wheeling a trolley. I glanced back at the plane and saw Trudy, on a stretcher, being carried down the gangway. I ran over, "Whatever's wrong, where are you taking her?"

"Keep your distance lady," the orderly yelled at me. "Suspected case of typhoid, there's an ambulance waiting."

Two air hostesses followed the stretcher complaining loudly: "What a fiasco. The stupid woman should never have boarded."

"Yeah and we had to give up our toilet just for her convenience. Some people have no sense or consideration."

"Not to mention the health risk she's posed to everyone even if it is only a virus. If it's Typhoid there'll be hell to pay. Those aeroplanes are one big incubator when it comes to bugs."

I finally met up with Harry and Jerome when all the hubbub had died down and we'd made it through customs. Harry, practically frothing at the mouth, verbally attacked me: "Where the hell have you been? I thought you'd got lost in the airport, and we'd left you behind in bloody Singapore. And we sure could have done with some support. Jerry was worried out of his brain, Trudy being so sick."

Yeah, but you'd have left me behind without a backward glance, I thought, *you great git.*

"You've got more to worry about than where I've been, Harry

my love. If Trudy's got Typhoid Fever, you and you're friend Jerry could be the next victims, then you'll really have something to worry about!"

I guess I could be a victim too, I thought, *but who cares.* After my holiday ordeal, I was so glad to tread on Aussie soil and escape Big Jerry, a dose of Typhoid Fever seemed totally irrelevant.

Robin Giraudo

Christmas Sestined

Tell me pray the true meaning of Christmas
Is it waking early in the morning
To gaze upon a star glittered tree,
Watch toddlers mesmerised by bright baubles
Gently shaking fancy ribbon-bound gifts
And sharing long of the Christmas spirit?

Early you start, raising high your spirit
Planning the day that will be your Christmas
The careful selection of special gifts
To present upon the early morning
And carefully hang bright shiny baubles
And ladder lift the angel to the tree.

The family gathers joyful round the tree
Sing hymnic songs of the holy spirit
Stop and admire the bright shiny baubles
Lightly kiss and wish all Merry Christmas
Tell tales of being woken in the morning
By children eager to ply them with gifts.

But you know Christmas is not just the gifts
Just as it is not the star glittered tree
It is the gathering in the morning
To remember the lost holy spirit
And to celebrate his birth each Christmas
With songs and prayer and bright shiny baubles

I wish my Christmas had bright shiny baubles
The pleasance of family would be the gifts
As we join at the table at Christmas
We'd laugh and sing around the glittering tree
While Grandma sips her warm Christmas spirit
Like this, I would look forward to morning.

But sleeping late I avoid the morning
spurn the singing beside tarnished baubles
Cork up the bottle of heavy spirit
That blots out the day and smashes the gifts
By evening the angel falls from the tree
So swallowing pills I long shun Christmas.

But you saved my spirit that dark morning
Now share your Christmas, hang your bright baubles
Ply me with gifts, and I stand beneath your tree.

Helen Iles

The Magic of Christmas

There's a trail of silver across the sky
It's reindeer dust left when they fly
drawing Santa's sleigh around the world
on his Christmas run to every boy and girl.

This trail of silver left from feet
which dance across the night, discreet
in how they touch the earthy ground
careful lest they careless bound
on roofs and fall inside;
where there's not a place to hide.

And if you're good in silent phase
you might hear the prancing ways
of golden hooves upon your roof
and Santa with his jovial laugh
as down he slides to leave a gift
hung on your mantelpiece aloft.

And watching closely through the door
why, there's silver dust upon the floor
and looking out through window bright
there's silver dust across the night
as reindeer prance back to the sky
Give them a wave and say a soft Goodbye

And smiling know the silver trail
is not as told, a snail's trail
It's where Old Nick and reindeer pals
have visited the boys and gals
and know this silver's magic treat;
it's flying dust for reindeer feet.

Helen Iles

When Santa Comes

Part I

Storming out of Maxwell's Department Store into heavy pedestrian traffic, Charissa Ernshaw fumed. She was more than just a little upset for Mr Davenport would not give her her job back even though she had almost begged him. It was now one week to Christmas. Her bank account was empty and she had lived the last week on borrowed money. She was so angry she desperately wanted to cry, as all she could see as she barged along the crowded footpath, using her shoulder to clear a path for herself, was little Susie crying on Christmas morning, sniffling as she watched the children playing on the street, each displaying new Christmas toys.

There would be no toys for Susie this year: there wouldn't even be a Christmas tree. But she fought hard not to cry, for life as a single 'mum' had toughened her to the hardships one had to constantly face. Why, only this morning she had tried to remind Susie that Santa might not make it to their house this year, trying to broach the subject each time it was subtly raised.

"Yes, he uses reindeer in the North Pole," she had nodded to Susie's question, "because the sled slides freely on the snow."

"But what if there is no snow."

She had to think quickly about that one, as she'd had to learn to do to a lot of Susie's questions lately. "Well, in Australia I believe he uses camels because the desert's far too hot for his reindeer."

Susie had sat and pondered that for a moment. "What if …"

"He uses elephants in India, and zebra in Africa. Can you

imagine Santa on a zebra?" Now how could she explain his lack of appearance this year; what could he not have to get him to their house. She couldn't think of a single thing, unless he broke down.

Charissa eased back in the crowd a moment, letting through an old woman who was jostled along in the swirling mass. The slightest touch would topple the old lady over, the highly polished cane doing little to help her unsteady legs in the unconcerned crush.

"Why don't people care anymore?" Charissa thought tetchily. "They could easily clear the way and move around her."

The old lady with watery grey eyes glanced up as she made her way past, the clearance Charissa offering her giving a few relieved steps in the rush. When the woman had moved on Charissa resumed her place, her shoulders ready to block and push as needed as she headed back on course. She had one last chance at Christmas, at buying a toy for Susie. Maybe The Arches would be taking on casuals over the Christmas rush. She had served burgers often enough at home to do it for a living.

'Just don't give up,' she impressed on herself as she reached the cross road. 'You have to keep trying, for Susie.'

Heavy traffic choked the cross-walk, and she took the moment to swallow back the hard lump in her throat. 'Whatever happens, you don't have to tolerate Mr Davenport and his kind putting their hands where you don't want them. Just because you have a child to raise on your own doesn't mean –'

The traffic cleared and she shot across the intersection ahead of everyone else, almost breaking into a run lest someone ask for a job ahead of her, lest someone take the only job available. "Dear God, let something happen so Susie will be happy. Anything. I'll do absolutely anything."

As soon as the words were out Charissa realised it was a long time since she had prayed. She had prayed often once, a long time ago, many many times in fact, but God had never answered her. 'So why would he now?' The lump climbed back to her throat and grew tighter. There was just one week to Christmas.

Opening the door to the burger bar, Charissa's jaw dropped open. It was as if her prayer had been answered. On the counter by the cash register was a big square sign. It read: "CASUAL WANTED. APPLY WITHIN."

Though the burger bar was nearly empty at this mid-afternoon hour, three girls stood at the counter, one fingering the sign as she spoke to the young man behind it.

'Oh, please no,' thought Charissa, fearfully. 'Oh, please don't do this to me.'

Every time that something looked slightly brighter for her, something always happened to knock her down again. This, it seemed, was just another of those times, yet what always made it crueller was that hope was dangled before being snatched away. She had long ago titled her life as one gigantic tease and had often wondered what terrible things she had done in her past to be so ruthlessly punished.

With large violet eyes, she watched as the three girls turned from the counter, the tallest one saying with a shrug as she passed, "I wouldn't mind, but it's just too close to Christmas. I want to have some fun at least for a while."

Charissa breathed easier and approached the counter, aware that the man was eyeing her up and down. She knew she was attractive, that her blonde spiralling hair accentuated a smooth, olive complexion and she had never needed to diet to maintain her slender shape – having Susie at such a young age had definitely advantaged her on that score.

She went forward smiling, delivering a carefully dealt dose of self-confidence. "Good afternoon," she said, sounding quite professional, "I would like to apply for the position you have advertised."

The man smiled immediately, yet with less lecherousness than Mr Davenport. Charissa felt hopeful. The man ushered her behind the counter and led the way to a small office at the end of the long silver kitchen. Tommy, he had told her his name was, left her with the manager, a much older and greyer version of male authority, yet his smile was the same as Tommy's.

Ten minutes later Charissa came out of the office, beaming and thanking God. She would start tomorrow. And if Mrs Bodakin could look after Susie till late in the evenings, she could work double shifts. She would soon be back on her feet – sooner than she had ever thought possible, she would have Mrs Bodakin paid back. Life was glorious!

Her step much lighter, she thanked Tommy heartily, instigating his broad grin and laughter. He had a pleasant face, she thought as she reciprocated his look. She was over the moon, and on the way home would have a look in the toy shop at that doll Susie always wanted. Her prayers finally answered she would never lose faith again.

'Everything is always for a reason,' she reminded herself, firmly believing it as she turned and waved Tommy goodbye. "See you tomorrow," she called.

Then it happened.

As she turned to her line of travel, she connected with something solid and was thrown totally off balance. The sudden overwhelming impact knocked her backwards, reeling her back so hard she flayed her arms to grasp anything that might halt her fall. Her fingers almost snared bare flesh, then lost their grip and she twisted and toppled sideways against a table. The table moved, scraped noisily along the floor, suspending her for a moment. Then all that was there was a chair, which toppled as she crashed to the ground.

Dazed, for it was over so quickly, she did not know what hat happened. She glanced up as a tall man bent down over her. Broadly built and dressed black t-shirt and jeans, his black pointy boots with silver studs filled her vision as she glanced back to where she was sitting.

"You should watch where you're going," he said as a broad tanned hand reached down to help her up.

Stunned, Charissa fought to keep cool at the man's impertinence. Exhaling long and hard, she looked up and clenched her teeth, warning herself that life was too good to ruin it by flinging her own assessment of the event. This was a customer. Inwardly seething, she glared at the broad squared chin and solid jaw, at the pair of pitch-dark eyes and the warm smiling mouth that bore down over her. The man's crop of thick wavy hair was darker than his eyes, yet not as dark as the shadow on his jawline. It seemed it had missed a razor for several long days.

"I … I'm sorry," she said as she reached up to take his hand. She tried to return to her feet as elegantly as possible, but his hand so firm and warm on hers distracted her thoughts. Taken by its smooth touch, she did not immediately feel the pain erupting in her left foot as it took her weight.

"Owwww!" she suddenly wailed. Buckling, she almost fell to the floor again, but two strong arms reached around her and lifted her, supported her while Tommy swung a chair around for her to sit on.

"Owww! It's my foot. My foot!"

Easing her to the seat, the darkly dressed man crouched before her and gently removed her court shoe. Charissa leant forward to view the damage, barely aware of the stranger's hand caressing her stockinged leg. Her heart hammered as the pain became apparent, as long brown fingers probed the swelling that had started in her ankle. Tommy disappeared from the room.

Placing his dark sunglasses on the table beside her, the man looked up at her. "You've broken your ankle," he said, shaking his head with regret.

Her grief was immediate, instant and barely containable as Charissa saw the hope whipped away. When Mr Tuckey, her new boss, arrived a second later he looked just as grim. How could she work now with a broken ankle? Charissa thought in dismay.

Pained violet eyes flicked over the man who had assailed her. Rough, unshaven, dressed entirely in black, only the silver buckle and studs of his belt and boots adding colour to his malevolence, he reminded her of the devil. Who else could undo her prayers!

"It can't be broken!" she protested. "This just isn't happening." This just couldn't happen to Susie. She didn't deserve this blow!

She tried to stand. "And what would you know anyway, you … you Hell's Angel cast-off!" she bellowed as she spotted the leather jacket he had tossed onto a chair.

He looked at her harshly as pain jolted up her leg again and stabbed like a wound into her groin.

"Aaaah." She collapsed back to the chair.

"Believe me, it's broken," he said most calmly, which annoyed her even further. "We had better get you to a hospital," he said, turning to the manager.

Helen Iles

When Santa Comes

Part II

Thirty minutes later, during which time the man had supported her, splinted her foot and carried her to the waiting ambulance, Charissa sat in a hospital room. Ice packs were wrapped around her very bruised ankle in an effort to reduce the swelling and pain, yet they could not reduce her tears now Susie was robbed of Christmas. It would be humiliating enough to borrow money from friends to feed her.

She lay back against white pillows, her eyes red from crying, while deep inside her head throbbed the annoying knowledge that Susie would be far better off in foster care. She had battled it out year after year, always wondering what life would have been if Donnie hadn't been killed in a car accident shortly after she had fallen pregnant. And she wondered if things would have been different if her parents had realised her love for him and not forbidden them to be together. "God, things could have been so different."

Another flood of tears washed her face, and she covered her eyes with her hands as the door slowly opened. She didn't like people seeing her so despondent. Usually she locked herself inside her room until sufficient composure was regained to stand up and fight again. But this time she had no privacy, and she wished the nurses would just bugger off and let her foot fall off for good.

"Does it really hurt that much?"

Charissa looked up and brushed the trickling tears from her cheeks with slender fingers. The man from The Arches stood at the foot of the bed, as handsome as a film star, as brashly confident as one, his jacket clutched in one hand, his sunglasses nestled in the other. Dark eyes cast a swift glance over her then settled on her foot.

"Yes." She couldn't help snapping. For once she felt she had a reason to take her misfortune out on someone else. And it was he who had shattered her hopes. It was he who had destroyed her faith in life. She would never forgive him. And she would never forgive the world, the universe or God for depriving Susie again. Susie, it seemed, the Lord had forgotten; she had suffered as much, if not more, than she.

The man dropped his jacket and glasses onto the chair beside her. "It shouldn't," he said. "They've given you a shot for the pain, haven't they?" Those long broad fingers probed her skin again just below the ice pack.

"Keep your hands off," Charissa snapped at him again. Sullen and cross, her resolve rekindled her anger.

"Well, have they?" One dark eyebrow lifted with the question.

"Yes. Ten minutes ago."

"Then it's obviously not working yet."

"May I ask what you are doing here?" Charissa didn't want him standing so close to her, seeing it was he who had put her here. "Or are you going to break my other foot?"

He cast her a bemused glance, then returned his attention to her foot. "Hey, it was you who ran into me, remember?" He cast her a sideways glance. "Or is something else bothering your pretty little head other than your foot?"

Looking away, Charissa shook her head. Her problems were her own, and his question made her feel mean for taking them out on him. Deeply, she wished he would return her animosity to make it feel all right. Instead, she repeated, "I asked what you were doing here."

He glanced at her face again, the swelling of her broken ankle seeming to fascinate him more. "I guess I came to see what else I could do for you, seeing you won't let me touch you, and seeing it was I you ran into and all. Can I notify anyone that you're here? Husband? Family?"

Charissa shook her head. "There's just my daughter. She will be worried if I'm late to pick her up."

The long fingers toyed again near the wrap of the ice pack, then caressed the ends of her toes that protruded through the cover. "You have a daughter?" He sounded surprised. But then again, Charissa remembered, she was only twenty-two, and barely looked eighteen.

She nodded, riling again. The pressure he was putting on her toes was starting to hurt. "She's six, and at that age she worries. She won't be having Christmas now because of this." She just couldn't hold the words in any longer. For once she didn't want to bear the painful disappointment alone. "I'd just got that job which would have changed everything. Now she won't even have a tree. Will you stop doing that! It damn well hurts."

She shot a stern glare his way as his fingers bent her toes slightly back.

"Who have you got who can pick her up, seeing there is no way you are able to?" He moved around to the side of the bed.

Charissa shook her head. How could she say there was no-one. Her life, apart from Mrs Bodakin who lived upstairs and was staying in Salisbury tonight, was just her and Susie.

She heard him sigh. Her problem was becoming tedious. "I guess I could pick her up if you want. I could bring her here for you." The dark sultry eyes glanced down at her.

"You've got to be joking!" Charissa erupted. You think I would entrust my daughter to a great hulking bikie! What sort of mother do you think I am?"

She hoped she wasn't jumping the gun with her accusations here, but the painted emblem she had glimpsed on the back of his jacket, the dark shades, the black Harley Davidson that had been parked outside the burger bar were far too coincidental. She caught the man's wry smirk as he stared back at her toes. "A very good one I guess, seeing you'd want to work in a burger bar to make sure she gets her Christmas." The words were delivered without looking up. "And I understand. Maybe I could arrange for someone else to collect her. One of the doctors here maybe?" Still he didn't look at her.

Charissa shook her head. It wouldn't be that easy. Yet she had to do something, for it was nearly time for Susie to be coming out of school and she didn't want her left waiting on the pavement. What the hell was she to do? She realised the man was only trying to help, but his suggestion to collect Susie was ludicrous.

She looked up and found him looking down at her, waiting for an answer. "It's not that simple," she admitted, speaking less tersely this time. "Susie has requirements; she needs special transport."

The man cocked his head.

"Susie's in a wheelchair. She broke her back when a balcony collapsed where we were living several years ago. I generally meet her after school and walk her home."

The man nodded, his lips thinning as he heeded the information. "I'm sure we can work something out," he said. Absently he handed her the phone from the room's side cabinet. "You'd better ring her school and tell them there will be a change of plans today."

Astounded at his common-sense, Charissa dialled the School of Little Shepherds and arranged that Mrs Hollingsgate would wait at the front of the school until Susie was safely collected. What else could she do? Charissa thought, defeated. She could only pray that God would protect her little girl now thrust into the hands of strangers.

Then her mood fell further as she realised she would soon be telling Susie that Santa would not be coming this year. His reindeer were far too tired; the sleigh got bogged in the snow. The camel couldn't stand the city traffic. Her luck had totally run out.

No, there would be no fake Santa snow flicked across the logs in the fireplace when she awoke on Christmas morning. No few presents stacked beneath the mantle. There would be no Santa at all.

Maybe this was the year she would tell her Santa didn't exist. Which was better than letting her think she had missed out on Christmas because she was a bad girl.

She looked up, fought back tears rising in her eyes and noted that the door was opening again. This time a white-coated blond-haired doctor entered. He flashed her a warm smile, glanced across the room at her visitor then moved around the bed to examine her foot. The dark-haired man moved away, folded his arms across his chest as the doctor prodded and squeezed Charissa's leg with his thumb and first finger. The doctor's smile increased as he flicked another glance across the room.

"So, Nick, what's this I hear about you creating patients to stem our minor slump. I thought we all agreed we were enjoying the rest."

The dark-haired man's jaw crossed and his lips pursed.

"What did you do? Tip her off the bike?"

Charissa glanced from one man to the other, slightly floored they knew each other. Inwardly she was highly amused at the bikie's expression; he was unimpressed at being accused of hurting her. She watched his dark eyes hood as his gaze dropped floorward, then it lifted to view her again.

"No, she fell," he said, stepping forward. Glancing briefly over her again, he said, "I have to go and organise getting her daughter home."

"You have a daughter?" the doctor said as the bikie left the room. He glanced at the closing door. "Have no fear, Doctor Goodfellow will bring her safely home."

Five days later, on a dusky Christmas eve, Susie sat at the large-paned window overlooking the street. Her deep blue eyes widened at the activity going on outside.

"Mummy, mummy!" she suddenly cried, her eyes sparkling as she turned back to her mother. Charissa hobbled awkwardly from the kitchen, crutches tightly tucked into her armpits, her hands coated with icing sugar that had missed the gingerbread men. Across the table behind her was strewn an assortment of sweets and delicacies – peace-offerings Nick had bought and delivered for their Christmas meal. "It's Doctor Nick, Mummy."

Hobbling to the window, Charissa saw Nick coming up the path. She knew she had been right to tell Susie that Santa wouldn't be coming by sleigh this year; yet very wrong to warn that he might not come at all. He was so, so very busy. She knew now as Nick climbed the stairs, his crooked arms laden with brightly wrapped gifts, that Santa this year rode a motorbike.

Helen Iles

The Christmas Tree

The stained, tottering house still stands. I don't remember it any other way. The white paint is just about all gone from the picket fence, and the gate doesn't squeak now it's fallen off the hinges. The red brick path is like a mouthful of broken teeth in need of flossing. My childhood friend and I used to play hopscotch on the verandah over the missing boards. Remnants of blue paint on the flyscreen door frame curl like mud at the end of summer. The fallen bits have blown into the corner with years of autumn leaves. Although the dirty brass doorknob is wobbly, it still holds the door in place. Our Dalmatian used to go under the house through the missing front steps to wait in the cool until we returned. Mum always told us off when we got home with the dust and cobweb-laden pooch.

There's still a little track around the side of the house through the blowsy pink roses. We always went in through the glassless window. There used to be shards of glass in the frame, but they were removed years ago, and the paint had rubbed off from years of kids entering this way. Once we were inside, our eyes adjusted to the dimness. Some light did come through the dirty windows; however, most of it was from the skylight in the hall. The house smelled a little musty but not too bad for the long abandonment. The distressed and shredded carpet morphed into wonky carpet squares with long strings of nylon trailing into mouse holes.

Upstairs were three bedrooms. One of them was wallpapered with little farm scenes. The green of the tractor was pale and the baby chicks seemed like yellow stains near the mother hen. The black and white cows showed up the best where they lined up at the milking shed. The jolly farmer's dark pants and the blue of his check shirt could still be seen, although the red had bleached to pink. I found a baby's dummy there a long time ago. The perished rubber felt tacky in my hand. I always wondered what happened to the baby.

The most extraordinary thing was in the lounge room downstairs. A decorated Christmas tree stood in the corner. I don't know if it had been left behind or whether someone brought it in after the house was abandoned. Taller than me, there were fake pine needles on plastic branches. The tinsel, in various new and faded shades. draped from top to bottom. I think people had been decorating the tree for a long time before my friend and I started adding an ornament each year. I know other people did decorations because the tree branches drooped from the weight of them. Some of the adornment was handmade, and some were shop bought: tin soldiers, baubles, and such. Over time some decorations disappeared. The old ones. They were never left in the house so someone must have taken them away.

Today I have no trouble reaching the window sill, but I scrape my shin on the way in. Using my torch, to avoid the trip hazard of the strings of old carpet, I search for the Christmas tree. There it is in the corner. A little wonky, and a lot dusty, but still ornate. Even though I expect the decorations to be different, it seems so much smaller. Now the whole thing only comes up to my waist. I take the gold glitter-covered bauble from my handkerchief and place the ornament on the tree. It's next to a fake pine cone with a piece missing which is looking very worn and old. I take the decrepit object and put it in my pocket. Then, I climb out of the window and go next door to my home.

Kathleen Knight

Kyoto – The Heart of Japan

"Wow! They look like they go right up to the sky!"

I didn't think there was much that could instil wonder in young people these days, but the escalators at Kyoto station certainly proved me wrong; and I was to be proved wrong a number of times during the remainder of our short stay in this beautiful city.

We had just arrived by bullet train, a two-and-a-half hour journey from Tokyo, with twelve 16-year-old boys from a high school in Perth, where my daughter taught Japanese. I was lucky enough to be able to join her, and two other teachers, on this holiday trip to Japan.

Kyoto station is enormous, more like a small town, with its own hotel, theatre, museum, department store and shopping mall. Finding our way out of this mammoth structure, we followed our guide to the Kyoto Daini Tower Hotel, about a five-minute walk away. Wasting no time, we deposited our bags in our rooms and were straight out of the door to explore our surroundings.

First stop for the boys was the incredible Bic Camera electrical department store. More oohs! ahhs! And wows! This store is huge! A complete floor is devoted to computers, another to cameras of all shapes and sizes and yet another to TVs, video games and associated equipment; and that was only three floors. After wandering around this six-storey building for an hour, what better sight to meet our eyes than an assembly of massage chairs. There were about twenty of them, most already occupied by elderly customers. After scouring the rows for a couple of empty chairs, Julianne and I finally managed to relax and rejuvenate our poor feet before meeting the boys and their chaperones for dinner.

Meals here were always an adventure for me: so much to choose from and so cheap. Just about every second shop is a restaurant, some of them so small they are easy to miss. These are usually where the locals eat and often the most authentic. Definitely worth trying. If you're not into Japanese food there is always McDonalds or KFC, but sampling the traditional dishes is half the fun of experiencing life in Japan.

After dinner, the next place on our list was Kyoto Tower. Built on top of the Kyoto Tower Hotel, the tower is more than 100 m high with an observation deck providing a 360° view of Kyoto. Telescopes are strategically placed and fixed on the magnificent sights in the hills around the city. Apparently, on a clear day you can see Osaka, but we were there in the evening and were delighted to watch as the city lit up the thirty-six peaks of Higashiyama to cries of amazement from everyone on the deck. Built in 1964, the concept behind its characteristic shape is a lighthouse built to illuminate the landlocked city of Kyoto.

According to the tourist brochure, some of the locals disapprove of the tower, but many have welcomed both the tower and the station, considering them essential modern additions to the city, to ensure that it doesn't become culturally isolated from the rest of new Japan. One expert on Japan's past has even called the tower a 'stake through the heart'.

Back on ground level, we were ready for bed. But the boys had other ideas; they wanted to try karaoke. So, off we went to look for a place to sit and amuse ourselves, listening to each other sing, not always in tune. The Japanese love karaoke and we tried three places before finding a vacant booth. One hour later, we were out and on our way back to the hotel. We needed a good night's sleep to prepare for the next day's tour of the more traditional and cultural areas of Kyoto.

The ancient capital of Japan for about 1,000 years, until it was moved to Tokyo in 1867, Kyoto is considered the mother of culture within Japan. Many of the customs of old Japan are kept alive here, and it is not unusual to see men and women going about their daily life wearing traditional dress. It's said that it's impossible to know the real Japan without knowing Kyoto and for this reason it is often called "Japan's heartland".

Kyoto has hundreds of temples and gardens. There's even an 11-page walking map to show you how to get to them. So, next day our first choice was one of the most famous temples of Japan: Kiyomizudera (Pure Water Temple). It was built in 780 AD and, in 1944, the temple was added to the list of UNESCO world heritage sites. To get there, we took a 15-minute bus ride from Kyoto and then walked up the narrow hillside streets of Higashiyama, moving aside occasionally to make way for cars, which looked totally out of place in this centuries-old region of Kyoto.

Kiyomizudera stands in the wooded hills of eastern Kyoto and offers visitors a panoramic view over the city from its famous wooden terrace. Below the terrace, you can taste the spring water, which gives the temple its name, and which is said to have healing powers. We wandered through the temple and its grounds, mingling with other tourists, and Maikos, apprentice Geishas, who giggled with delight when asked to have photographs taken with us. The mood was spoilt a little when a couple of them took out cigarettes from their kimonos and started to smoke in front of us.

We finally began to make our way back down the narrow streets, stopping on the way to browse in the local shops for souvenirs. The Japanese shopkeepers were very friendly and helpful and we were grateful to the owner of a small kiosk who supplied us with ice and tissues to help stem the nosebleed of one of our boys.

After a quick lunch, next stop was Rokuon-Ji Temple, more popularly known as Kinkaku or Golden Pavilion, because it's literally covered in gold leaf. It's especially famous because the Buddha's ashes are enshrined here, and this is why the name

Kinkaku-ji is commonly used instead of Rokuon-ji.

In 1950 the Golden Pavilion was destroyed by a fire which was started by a priest and in 1956, the Japanese writer, Mishima Yukio wrote the famous novel Kinkaku-ji, based on this incident. He later committed suicide as a means of protest about the loss of traditional values in his country.

There was so much to see here, but the most amazing sight for me was the Kyoko-chi pond (mirror pond) which reflects the Golden Pavilion like a mirror, emphasizing the building, creating a peaceful atmosphere and making the magnificent Golden Pavilion shine even more.

Tired, but still in awe of the sights we'd seen, we made our way back to our hotel. Tomorrow was Thursday, next stop Hiroshima.

Val McCabe

Christmas Camping Holiday

"You right, Love?"

"Yep, I'm right."

"Then we're off and racing. Did you pack the esky? I bet you forgot the kids' toothbrushes? What about the reindeer ears? Got the thongs for the shower? And spare dunny rolls? I bet you forgot to pack them? And if you forgot the esky then you must have forgotten the snaggers and turkey legs for tea tonight. What about the Chrissy pudding? And the cold ones I had on standby in case of a road side emergency? You know we are bound to have one of those! Crikey, Love, petrol's gone up. Dodgy time to put it up, don't you reckon, over the Chrissy Hollies? Flaming multi nationals. Did you book the camp site and get confirmation on your mobile? You know how packed it gets at Chrissy! Oh no, don't tell me you forgot to download it onto your mobile. Geez, Love, can't you do anything? Did you lock the front door, put out the cat for Myrtle next door to feed, stop the newspaper deliveries for the week and empty the fridge? Did you remember Tyson's suppositories, the sunscreen and the Vicks Vapour rub? I'm not going anywhere without the Vicks. Do you think we've got enough tins of fruit salad? What about blankets in case it gets cold? Did you check the weather? Did you pack the kids bathers? Have you hidden the pressies properly? We can't have the kids discovering them early you know? I remember the time… Geez, Love, you're not even listening to me. You've got your blooming ear plugs in again. Now I'll have to go through the whole list again. Did you pack the esky?"

Elizabeth Pappas

Orthodox Easter Holiday

Chanters in churches courier the words
   of solemn ministers and padre.
Pronouncing to all the Julian calendar's date,
   time for another Orthodox Easter holiday.
Those who say they are not fashioned from potter's clay.
Remain unreceptive to God the unseen physician and stay away.
Puzzled by believers who gather in intimate crowds to pray.
Still the devout jostle finding hope beneath an apostolic gateway.
Harking back to times long ago
   when people held in their hands sprigs of basil spray.
Now catch upon a breeze smoky incense,
   frankincense and sweet bay.
Reviving century after century the substance
   of Easter's painful passion play.
Incense drifts upward escaping; floating lazily away.
Ecclesia walls covered in mosaics mimic the apex of the sun's rays
Portray saints' and bishops' halos reflected in gold and silver inlay.
They recall parables of biblical tales
   glistening in lights of curling candle ray.
Under Roman rule Easter's mystical story
   is repeated reeking of foul play.

Still the scriptures tell Jesus forgave
    and washed the sins of the world away.
And as forty days of fasting pass,
    feasting begins with scarlet eggs on display.
Christ has risen, Christ has risen devotees jubilantly say.
Wishing one another best wishes till next year's ascension day.

Elizabeth Pappas

Bygone Christmases

Where have you gone Christmases past?
I seek you in all the places we have ever known.
Where have you gone?
I search for you.
I ache for you but you aren't there anymore.
If I come another day will you be there?
If I twist, warp time for just a second, perhaps?
Will you be there?
If I leave as I know I must, will you be there after I am gone?
If I turn suddenly will you be there?
Oh, time, time.
If only I could shift time, so I can be with you.
Again.
Time and time again.
Time plays with my mind
And always around Christmas time.

Elizabeth Pappas

An Aussie Kazzie Chrissy

At Christmas time guess who's cooking calamari, katoumari and roast turkey?

In our Burswood home cloves, cinnamon and garlic hit you right on the nosey!

Pavlova, baklava, lemon and oregano chicken souvlaki.

Christmas at our house is like being back in Greece on the tiny island of Kazzie.

But with a unique twist cos this girl's an Aussie.

Our Kazzie Aussie family is blessed because we have two chances at Christmas frivolity.

We also celebrate a second Christmas on the 7th of January.

On either day knock on our door, move someone's toosh and grab a pozzy,

Hubby's playing Greek music loudly trying to do a Zorba Sirtaki.

He's all fired up by the sound of the booming bouzouki.

His eyes sparkle as he dances like a wild green-eyed Greek gypsy.

We all laugh cos his dance looks more like a silly two-step Watusi.

It's a day filled with peace so throw out your worries along with your komboloi

We wonder if Christmas day is meant to be spent acting righteous and holy?

Mmm, perhaps on this day we should behave.

Not eat the naughty foods which I have to admit I all too often crave.

You know the ones we are told will send us to an early grave?

I look out the window, there's definitely no snow.

So we won't need our crazy knitted reindeer jumpers Granny gave us all those years ago.

The sky is clear, the oven's full and sizzling hot, I reckon family and friends will devour the lot!

Oh, Lord and the weather forecasters say it's going to be over forty.

If we had a pool and no kids we'd pretend we were young again, skinny dip and be naughty.

But on this day under boughs of mistletoe kisses planted on cheeks is as far as respectable people go.

We all relax because we don't have to do the dishes.

God bless dishwashing machines invented for mums through millions of past Christmas wishes.

As the day wears on, it unbearably hot, everyone jostles seeking out the coolest spot.

The air's got smoky cos Hubby's fired up the barbie.

Everyone laughs cos my satay stick sauce is too lumpy.

We love this crazy day filled with affection, laughter and frivolity.

It's an Aussie Greek Christmas so chuck out anyone who's being grumpy.

Wearing reindeer ears we all shout out cheers, poke funny faces and behave mischievously.

I bring out the Xmas pudding flamed luminously blushing red with Metaxas brandy.

Hubby laughs and says "I've got the fire hose handy."

Then our pudding gets drowned in thick luscious cream from Peter's Dairy.

On this sacred day when Joseph comforted Mary.

One can't help but think of Jesus and his Mum Mary.

She was led to Bethlehem poised, vulnerable and pregnant on a donkey.

And the three wise men known as the Magi reveal to his parents

Jesus's glory.

Declaring to them that the child is holy.

His destiny foretold for he is the son of God Almighty.

Tiny he lay in a humble stable wrapped in strips of white swaddling.

Love and forgiveness to all who repent his sacred calling.

Through his legacy he brings blessings and hope to all humanity.

He guides all peoples on earth to seek goodwill, world peace and universal harmony.

On this sacred day let's open our hearts and be a God Groupie.

For I have found in all things Christ's wisdom worthy of thanksgiving.

He's like Moses, Buddha, Mohamad, the Dali Lama and Ghandi.

They preached love, and justice is for all humanity, not just those with power and wealth in our society.

They believe it's a sin to wage war, not care for the disenfranchised, the homeless, hungry and lonely.

These men know we can make a better world if we reflect wisely and behave more kindly.

So today and any other day let's not argue who's right or wrong about the Koran, the Torah or any other standpoint on theology.

In the face of religious conflict let's stop bickering for our children's safety, world stability, humanities continuity.

Let's seek first to understand as our great teachers did, forgive the past cos that's now history.

Focus on making our future non-violent, fair for all, creating a blissful universal epiphany.

For if we look deeply into the hearts of all people we will find great beauty.

On Christ's birthday let's reflect on love and peace, make that human kind's essential victory

And so on this hopeful note, love and best wishes everybody from this Aussie Kazzie family.

Definitions

"Kazzie" is an affectionate term for Kastellorizians. "Kazzies" are part of Greek community of Australia. Many Kastellorizians migrated to Australia, especially WA, during the late 19th century and throughout the early to mid-20th century. Kastellorizo is located 4kms off the Turkish mainland of Anatolia. Katoumari (traditional Kastellorizian sweet), calamari (squid), baklava (Greek sweet), oregano (wild herb used to flavour meats), souvlaki (shish kabab), toosh (bottom), pozzy (seat), komboloi (Greek worry beads).

Elizabeth Pappas

Santa's Crisis

A week before Christmas
Santa had a great fright
When he gazed in the mirror
Not a hair was in sight.

He called Mrs Claus
Who had a great notion
She poured on his head
Some hair raising lotion.

But it must have been X brand
Because it turned out a shocker
His hair grew so wildly
He looked like a Rocker.

He played at a few gigs
But it wasn't his style
Moaning I'll cut off my hair
And stay home for a while.

But his fans sent him presents
Satin pants with pink bows
Chanting our Santa's a cool dude
Put on some more shows.

So he stuck cotton wool
All over his head
But it stuck out in tufts
And turned his skin red.

His reindeer tried singing
Crooning outside his shack
While elves polished his head
But not a hair would grow back.

Poor Santa was sobbing
I can't go out tonight
A bald headed Santa
Will give children a fright.

He felt himself sweating
And gave out a scream
He'd fallen out of his bed
It was just a bad dream.

He put on his red suit
And brushed his white hair
Then set off in his sleigh
Without a bald Santa care.

Enis Pearce

Santa's Warning

It's not the twinkle in your eye
It's the tilt of your tum as you wobble by
You've had too many pies
And too many ales
To sound surprised at the voice of the scales.

You're a diet free Santa
Who cannot say no
And leave behind cake crumbs
Wherever you go.

Your reindeers are worried
They won't lift in the air
So remember dear Santa
All food you must share.

Enis Pearce

Ye Olde Village

Under a deep indigo sky Snowville's tiny houses lay snuggled in a soft blanket of snow.

During the year nothing ever changed. The temperature didn't alter, the sky remained clear, and the snow never melted leaving a soft crunch underfoot as the villagers went about their business. All in all, it resembled a picture of contentment and so it was until the dreaded time of the year arrived. CHRISTMAS!

Christmas and the once sleepy village was abuzz with activity. The expressions on the villagers' faces however, were not ones of joy. The lights of the only Toyshop were out and the queue to the apothecary's door stretched as far as the outlying fields.

Inside the tiny chemist shop, Mr Jenkins the apothecary worked feverishly stirring different coloured potions into large bowls labelled 'Adults', 'Children', and 'Babies'.

He tut-tutted as he stared out through the window and saw the ever growing line.

"Come over here, Marty," he called to his young apprentice. "I need you to help me siphon this medicine into those bottles." He pointed to where boxes of empty bottles were stacked by the wall. "Quick, lad, or we'll be running out of time."

Marty needed no second bidding; he knew what the consequences would be.

A few minutes later he stood beside Mr. Jenkins who siphoned the mixtures into the bottles whilst he corked them and stuck on the dosage labels. The lined up bottles made a colourful display, bright red for the adults, to avoid the danger of a wrong mixture being given to those too young. Bright blue for the children to make it look more enticing – though sadly that didn't work once they'd tasted it – and pink for the babies. They finished not a moment too soon with the jangle of the front door announcing the arrival of their first customer. This was not surprising since Mr Jenkins had looked at his watch in horror a minute ago and raced to turn his closed sign to open.

A young woman with two young children and nursing a baby came in and approached the counter.

"Hello, Mrs Plum," he greeted her. "I guess you'll need an extra bottle this year," he nodded his head towards the baby she held in her arms.

"Oh yes please," she replied, "I'll need three bottles. One for my husband and me, one for the children to share, and the other for baby Mickey." Her voice started to falter. "I … I … hope he will be alright. It's his first Christmas, you see."

He smiled reassuringly at her. " Don't worry yourself, Mrs Plum. You've managed well with your other two, haven't you?"

She smiled weakly back at him. "I guess so … it hasn't been easy."

"No," he said sympathetically, "at this time of year it can't be easy on all you mothers and fathers. Now pass me your basket and I'll pack your bottles safely for you."

With the basket firmly placed on the counter, the two elder children watched him with great interest, until they saw him place the three coloured bottles into it, at which they immediately began to cry.

Tommy, the tallest one, tried to tug free from the hand of his mother and cried out. "Oh no Mum! Is it Christmas again? I hate Christmas … it always makes me sick."

Georgie, his brother, made a bolt for the door yelling. "I don't want to be sick; I don't want to be sick again."

Luckily for Mrs Plum, Marty had managed to plant himself in

front of the door to prevent Georgie getting out. Distressed as she was, she tried to coax the two boys.

"Come on, boys. It will soon be over and I've bought a big jar of barley sugar sticks for you to suck on. You like those, don't you?"

Georgie snivelled. "S'pose."

Spurred on by this better response, she continued, "C'mon then, boys, let's get home. We have much to do. We have to check everything is strapped down and make sure our seat belts still work properly."

As they tried to emerge, Mrs Button from the drapery shop pushed past them and called out to Mr Jenkins. "Any chance of a bottle for my cat and dog this year?" He heaved a sigh.

"No, sorry, Mrs Button. With all the births in the village this year supplies are running low, so all the animals will have to fend for themselves. I think most of the villagers are keeping theirs in a shed with plenty of hay to stop them getting hurt if they're thrown about and also to make it easier to clean up If they're sick."

"Okay, fine – I'll take mine," she snapped, and held out her hand for the bottle he was holding. "What about Mr Farmer? Have you enough spare for his cows?"

"No, they'll have to suffer like the rest."

She scowled. "You mean we'll be drinking curdled milk again for the next few weeks?"

Mr Jenkins grimaced. "Afraid so." The door nearly jangled off its hinges as she left his premises.

Mr Jenkins shook his head and sighed as the next customer entered. It was going to be a long day.

As the line to the Apothecary depleted the sound of nails being hammered into walls could be heard throughout the village. Mr Fuzzlewick, the Mayor, was making his customary rounds of its inhabitants to ensure they were well stocked up with food and clothing before the frequent falls of snow began. Everybody knew that venturing outside once the blizzards began could be extremely dangerous. Mr. Postie had learnt his lesson the hard way a couple of years ago. He'd run out of bread and tried to go next door to see if they had some to spare. Unluckily for him the blizzard arrived at the same time he stepped outside. It was pure chance his neighbour had glanced out through the window when it finished and recognised his blue boots sticking up in the snow. By the time he was pulled out the colour of his skin matched his boots. It would have been a different outcome if another blizzard had immediately followed for his boots would have been completely covered over.

His final call was to Mr. and Mrs Plum's house, where he found the father, Joe Plum, putting the last touches to straps inside chairs, which were chained to the wall.

"Okay children, Joe called, "come and try your seatbelts." He'd no sooner strapped them in when the house shuddered.

"Oh no!" Mrs. Plum screamed, "Christmas has come early."

Joe grabbed her and the baby who was tied to her and strapped her in a chair too.

"Come on, Mr. Fuzzlewick," he yelled, "there's a spare chair here for you."

Within seconds of Joe strapping himself in, the whole room shook. Suddenly they found themselves hanging upside down, then upright again. Immediately it stopped, they all threw up, and the children cried, " We hate Christmas, it makes us feel sick."

They had no sooner got the words out of their mouths when another shudder came and they were upside down again then once more in the righted position. The children were now sobbing. "Suck on your barley sugar sticks," said Mrs. Plum, "until I can be sure it's safe to get up to give you some medicine."

"Yes, we'd better give it a few moments," said Mr Fuzzlewick, "to see if we shake side to side because it's shortly after that we have the blizzard."

***

In another World a little girl gazed into a glass dome she held in her hand. “Look, Mummy,” she said, “isn’t it a beautiful village? I wonder what it’s like to live there? I’ll send them some more snow, they’ll probably like that.” She shook the dome furiously from side to side, tipped it upside down then back. She watched the snow swirl then settle.

A smile of contentment crossed her face as she looked up at her mother and said: “Doesn’t it look beautiful, Mummy? I love it when it’s Christmas, don’t you?”

Enis Pearce

A Glance at the Baltic Region

Never would I have thought I'd be boarding a ship again after having experienced debilitating seasickness when young. But here I am, on my way to the Baltic Sea eager to discover this much-extolled region.

Today we are sailing the North Sea. The 'Rotterdam' glides smoothly on; the sky is of a grey hue, the sea mirrors it. All is calm. We'll be at sea for a whole day before reaching Copenhagen. But boredom is not on the ship's menu. This gracious lady has much to offer in way of entertainment. From music to cooking demonstrations to movies; there are speciality restaurants, a theatre where variety shows are performed each night, a casino, swimming pool and much more. Arts and antiques decorate walls and passages where guests can stop and admire at leisure. The library sports a spacious lounge. Here passengers can sit and read their preferred book, watch the relaxing view as the ocean drifts by or play library games and quizzes. The atmosphere of the whole setting is very pleasant indeed. Coffees and drinks are always available on order.

Copenhagen, the first port of call, greets us with misty but fairly good weather. The booked excursion takes a group of us passengers directly to where the 'Little Mermaid' graciously sits on a boulder by the water's front. This genteel looking bronze figure, popular worldwide, is inspired by one of Hans Christian Andersen's famous fairy tales. Since 1913, when the iconic statue was unveiled, it has been vandalised several times. But now here she is, in all her loveliness, and admired by millions of visitors.

Copenhagen's unique and picturesque styles of buildings with their variety of bright colours must have contributed to Hans Christian Andersen stories and fairy tales. We leisurely cruise the canals of this tidy city under a gentle sunshine taking with us a most pleasant experience.

Denmark's royal residence in Copenhagen shines in its simplicity and architectural style. On listening to the guide's talk on the royals' traits and lifestyle one can discern that they are much-loved and respected by the general public.

Warnenmunde: At this German port town, the excursion I booked in advance is cancelled. What to do? The small seaside resort is at walking distance from where the ship is docked. With two companions, I venture on foot among old, quaint buildings where many windows sport dainty plants and flowers; there's hardly a car passing by. We roam around under a lenient sky admiring this particular part of town that reminds me of old, carefree times when the world wasn't spinning at as fast a pace as it nowadays is. A shop with myriads of mostly small rectangular boxes brimming with greens and flowers on display outdoors attracts my attention. As I browse inside the shop I feel as if I'm in a fairyland. On stands, on walls, on the ground and hanging from the ceiling dainty outdoors and indoors figurines and baubles mingle with plants and flowers, clever lighting enhances the fantasy sensation. Further on, we stop at a cafe for delicious, large cappuccinos: a day to look back on.

Tallinn is the place to be for the lover of architecture for it belongs to a long changeable history. Denmark, Sweden, Russia, Germany, all left their mark. The many different styles of architecture stand side by side, complementing one another. The lower city centre has been generally restored to a vibrant outlook; medieval buildings whisper of old times gone by.

Menacing grey clouds hover above. This doesn't stop tourists from pouring in as the day wears on. At a souvenir shop, where amber artefacts and ornaments abound, there's a compartment stacked with thick woollen gloves, beanies and socks, telling me of icy cold winters.

Recently Tallinn was awarded the cleanest city in Europe. A well deserved token.

St. Petersburg, a city sought by many travellers, has a lot to offer, from architectural wonders to a past steeped in history. St. Petersburg, founded by Peter the Great in the early 1700s, served as a defence post to fend off the marauding Swedish. In its three centuries of existence it has seen many changes and many rulers.

Today I'm at the incomparable Winter Palace. As I enter the first great hall I'm astounded at what I see: every gilded decoration, every marble and gilded statue, every nuance is of the most exquisite and finest artwork I've ever seen.

In general, the architecture of St. Petersburg reminds me of European cities; its clean canals and tidy city is an asset to the place.

Yesterday, at Catherine Palace, I enjoyed more outstanding architecture and brilliant art; the famous 'amber room' holds a beauty of its own. The palace is surrounded by lovely gardens where one feels at peace wandering the shaded paths.

Helsinki. Like St. Petersburg architecture, Helsinki's is very much European. Finland has been under foreign rules for centuries. In 1917 it declared independence, which is enjoyed to this day. Our tour guide, a gentle and caring person, tells us that Finnish people love their earned independence.

Today, after a tour of this lovely, relaxed city, we are bound to Sibelius Park where the impressive monument in honour to the famous Finish composer stands. I'm quite taken by this huge structure based on steel pipes welded together in a wave-like pattern. Most of the 600 pipes are embossed with exquisite designs.

The whole concept is of a uniform silvery colour. It's a pleasure to walk about the park for its semi- natural condition makes one feel close to nature.

Stockholm. The sun accompanies us on our first day of this city of islands. The coach meanders between greenery and lovely buildings, some with an affinity to Paris's architectural style. Road traffic is orderly. The highlight of the day is the Golden Hall at Stockholm City Hall. Forty-four metres long, its walls are encrusted with colourful mosaics depicting allegories and artistic arrangements: a marvellous ensemble of man's imagination.

At an old part of the city, narrow cobbled lanes flanked by old tall buildings slope head-down. Here I picture a Nordic winter when snow falls freely and ice forms on the ground – a slippery combination.

On the following day we are taken to 'Vasa Museum'. The place is filled with people marvelling at what they witness, I too stand there in amazement. I never expected this 17th century ship to be so huge, so impressive. Its meticulous restoration gives a vivid insight of its original state. I see it more as a work of art than a battle ship as it was meant to be. The Vasa never had a chance to fight a battle for it sank soon after it was launched due to uncalculated counterbalance.

We leave port on a chilly but fine morning. Wrapped up in warm clothes, I stand at the stern with other passengers watching the many wooded islands that dot the Swedish coast pass by; a perfect place for summer holiday. Visiting Stockholm has been great. The city and its people exude friendliness.

Aarhus: Today we're driven to Silkeborg to see the amazingly well-preserved 'Bog Man', as it's familiarly called. The remains are kept in a glass casket, a beam of light aims at its features allowing the viewer to see it in detail, the fairly young, peaceful-looking face tells of a natural death. The exhibit is well worth the trip.

We drive on to the Highland Lakes of Denmark. Here one can sit and relax, letting time flit by while enjoying a panorama of nature's inimitable beauty.

Time is up. We are now on the North Sea heading for Rotterdam, the port of our departure. I've enjoyed the most satisfying journey that will stay with me for a long, long time.

It's the last day of June – and what a glorious day it is, sky and sea complement each other. No seasickness this time in the two weeks of sailing, my prescribed tablets to counter the malady are still intact in their box. Like the first day of sailing, I sit by my cabin's window contemplating the movements of the great waters of the ocean – bewitching …

Silvana Preo.

Labelled

Christmas morning dawned dark over a town that appeared resentful of the thin sunbeams fingering its dark corners with colour. Outside the house at 10 Burton Street it was similarly bleak. Here, drifts of snow piled thickly against the walls, driven by winds so cold that ice formed the top layer like cake frosting. News flashes warned drivers in Kent and the southern counties to take special care on roads that were slick and treacherous. While no sudden shift in these weather conditions was heralded, inside the house it was a different matter. Inside the house, change was on its way. Here, a five-year-old was about to plan a double murder, which would then lead to the solving of a cold case, which would later lead to two people committing themselves to the eradication of violence and prejudice against women. To the uninformed, the link between the prevailing weather conditions and these three elements may appear tenuous, but this is not the case. One thing leads to another, as they say. Please, let me explain.

At 7 o'clock that same morning, two small children, one five and one six, were permitted to enter their parents' upstairs bedroom. They were wished happy Christmas by loving parents who, in the joy of gift distribution, failed to observe the change in their daughter's facial expression. So let us, as observers, voyeurs even, take a closer look. The edges of the little girl's mouth, which a moment ago had turned upwards, are now turned down. Her eyes, which had sparkled in anticipation, now sparkle with tears. Their six-year-old son, on the other hand, maintains the expression of a happy child, well satisfied. One youngster is passed the handle of a small grey pushchair, the other the handle of a shiny green bicycle. I will not tell you, dear reader, which child receives which gift, for that you already know.

On her return downstairs, Maddie put on a brave front. For her parents' sake, she smiled through breakfast and she smiled through lunch. She pulled bonbons, she shared jokes, she ate a little turkey. Let me tell you, it was an Oscar performance. Then she found that was the very best she could do, feeling the way she did, and she excused herself from the table.

"She's gone to play with her dolls," her mother explained, smiling brightly at those around the table. No-one expected her father to smile. Since the unsolved disappearance of his beloved only sister, Dora, seven years before, the fact was that her father had found little to smile about. The police had listed it as a cold case but this was hard for him to accept. Everyone at the table understood this. Nevertheless, he did his best.

Further down the table, Maddie's Uncle David (for your information, he's the one second from the left in the smart black leather jacket with the lustrous silver buttons) glanced quizzically at his young nephew, who avoided his eye. They clearly knew Maddie better than her parents did. Something was amiss.

Homemade Christmas pudding with brandy butter was served. "Delicious," murmured the guests.

"My mother's recipe," beamed Maddie's mother.

The conversation then turned to reminiscences of Christmases past, the sort of small talk that causes everyone not personally involved to stifle a yawn and to wish they were elsewhere. As outsiders ourselves, let us leave them to it and return to the five-year-old in question.

Having reached the sanctity of her bedroom, Maddie closed the door and wept. Why had Father Christmas ignored her letters? Why had he listened to James and not to her? Had she not been nice enough to measure up? She thought she had, yet dolls were the very worst present Saint Nick could have given her. She could not think of anything more boring. A beautiful bicycle like the one he had given James was all she had dreamt of for weeks. She had even told Jess, her best friend at school, that she would let her ride it. Now she would look foolish.

With no more tears to shed, Maddie wiped her eyes, forcing herself to face the two dolls. Dressed in pink gingham, they smiled glassily at her. She looked at the label attached to each one. Pauline. Patricia. She stuck out her tongue. "I hate you!" she hissed. Still that glazed smile. Beastly, boring dolls! She glanced at the thin summer dresses. How silly when it was so cold. Then she remembered. 'Exposure' – that was the word her teacher had used when she had warned them to wrap up well. Maddie looked out of the window at the snow, piled up almost to the windows. Prolonged exposure to the cold would kill anything, her teacher had said, even polar bears. Feeling more hopeful than she had all day, Maddie stood up and took the handle of the pushchair. This was the solution. It was that simple. She would tell her parents she had taken the dolls for a walk and simply forgotten where she had left them. She would cry. They would eventually find the bodies, feel sorry for her, dispose of the dead dolls and buy her a bicycle. She hoped it would be purple, with a flashing reflector on the back, like the one she had pointed out to her mother in the bicycle shop a week before Christmas.

Energised by her decision, it did not take long to execute. Soon the dolls, dragged through the snow in their pushchair, were wedged up behind the garden shed. Icicles had formed on the roof. They dripped slowly onto the snow, the pushchair, the dolls. By nightfall they would all have frozen. By the morning, Pauline and Patricia would have suffered prolonged exposure and that would be the end of them. Relieved, Maddie ran back inside and closed the door.

So much for the double murder, dear reader, but what about the cold case and the double commitment to eradicate violence and prejudice against women? Please, I beg you, be patient. Read on.

At first, Maddie didn't recognise the blonde woman sitting on her bed when she returned from the snow. Then she did.

"Aunt Dora!" she exclaimed. "I've seen you in photos. I didn't know you were coming for Christmas."

"Ah!" Her aunt laughed and hugged her. "It's a surprise. I'm missing, you know."

"Yes, my Dad told me. He can't smile any more. Where have you been?"

"I was murdered seven years ago. Tell your Dad I'm buried under the garage at number 25, just down the street. The man who did it killed himself but, as you know, Maddie, your Dad and the rest of the family still suffer." She stopped and looked sternly at her niece. "Believe me, Maddie, murder isn't the way to go."

Guilt showed in Maddie's stricken face. She looked down at the carpet. "Okay," she whispered. "So what do you want me to do?"

Her aunt smiled. "That's more like it! Now, I want you to bring those dolls back in and tell your parents you want to talk to them; ask them both to stop labelling you. Tell them who you really are."

Maddie stared at her aunt. "Who I really am?"

"Yes. They've labelled you because you're a girl. My parents were the same and it's a sad mistake. You have your own personality. There's nothing wrong with being a girl, or a boy, who likes dolls. But you don't and they should know that. They should know *you*!"

Maddie shook her head. "But they say because I'm a girl it's natural that I'll like dolls. How am I going to make them understand it's not?"

Aunt Dora smiled. "Tell your father you know he once traded his train set for a teddy bear and he slept with it for years. I think it only went to the tip when he married your Mother!"

Maddie gasped. "My father had a teddy bear?"

Her aunt laughed. "Indeed he did. Now go and get those dolls!"

Maddie nodded. "Will you be here when …"

"No, I'll have gone when you get back. But tell your Dad I'm happy now, so he can smile again. And remember, I'll be keeping an eye on you and I never want you to accept any treatment that is given to you just because you're a girl. Do you promise me that?"

"I promise," said Maddie, reaching up and kissing her aunt on the cheek. "Thank you." Then she tiptoed from her bedroom and ran to retrieve the pushchair from behind the garden shed.

"Maddie", called her father. "You've been asleep for hours. It's late. Everyone's gone home."

"You must be hungry," said her mother. "Do you want to bring the dolls into the family room for tea?"

Maddie took a deep breath. She was only five-years-old, after all, and this took courage. She followed them both to the tea table.

"Mum, Dad, can I talk to you about the dolls?"

They stared at her in surprise.

"What about them?"

"They're not what I asked for and I'm not that sort of person."

She met their blank stares. "What do you mean, Maddie? All girls love dolls."

"No, they don't. And all boys don't love train sets either. Some of them prefer teddy bears." She looked pointedly at her father.

He coloured slightly. "Okay, Maddie. Who've you been talking to? What's this about?"

"Aunt Dora," she said.

"Are you mad!" her father gasped. "What are you saying? She's missing …"

"Yes, I know. She was murdered and she says you'll find her body under the garage at number 25," Maddie said quietly.

Her father gripped her shoulder hard. "Murdered! Number 25! Who's been putting this nonsense into your head?" he yelled.

"Just a minute, Don." His wife looked at Maddie. "What's this all about?"

"Aunt Dora stopped me murdering those dolls," she whispered, avoiding her mother's eye. "She said murder isn't a good way to go."

Her parents stared at her.

"You were going to murder your dolls!"

Maddie nodded mutely.

"I think you need to go to your room and we'll decide what to do about this, young lady," her mother said angrily. "Maybe the school counsellor can help you. I can't believe what I'm hearing!"

Maddie's father shook his head. "No, Penny. There's more to it. I did have a teddy bear and I did swap my train set for it."

His wife stared at him. "So what do you want to do?"

"Silly as it sounds, I'm going to speak to the police." He looked apologetic. "I wouldn't want to let Dora down."

"The child has a dream and you go to the police. I don't believe this!" Maddie's mother shook her head.

Maddie's father knelt down beside his daughter. "Did Aunt Dora say anything else?" he asked.

Maddie nodded. "She said she's happy now, so you can smile again."

Tears welled in his eyes and he nodded. "Anything else?"

Maddie looked at him. "Yes. She said she'll be keeping an eye on me and she never wants me to accept things that happen to me just because I'm a girl." She hesitated. "What will you do if the police find Aunt Dora's body, Dad?"

He took her hand and smiled. "We'll have a funeral for her at last and I'll work on getting to know my children better. Now what was it you wanted for Christmas?"

And so it was, dear reader, that Aunt Dora at last received the funeral she deserved, with Maddie riding alongside the coffin on a large purple bicycle with a flashing reflector while James rode behind the cortege on his bike of shiny green. You'll also be glad to hear that the dolls, Patricia and Pauline, found a home with a small girl who loved them dearly and never once thought of murdering them. It then follows, of course, that Maddie's father smiled often, and never again labelled anyone; indeed, in later life he stood alongside Maddie as they carried out vital work in the field of eradicating violence and prejudice against women. And needless to say, the story of that day has been told at Christmas lunch every year since then and hasn't bored anyone yet, not even those who were not personally involved.

Marilyn Rainier

Christmas Musings 2018

Urged to write on Christmas has made me think how I now regard this event and what I observe about Christmas in the first couple of decades of the 21st century. Yesterday I had, of necessity, to visit shops to buy Christmas cards and a few presents for an upcoming "Christmas wind-up." In fact, I have just participated in another of these events and have two more next week to attend and celebrate the drawing near of Christmas.

I say celebrate, but this is not really what we do. Basically they are parties where we catch up with friends and colleagues, eat too much, drink sometimes too much, laugh, give presents and generally come away feeling warm and having had a good time. But Christmas has very little to do with it. We may sport Santa Claus type hats, wear flashing earrings, T-shirts with Ho Ho Ho writ large, but Advent and Christmas have little to do with these celebrations.

Discussing Christmas family events with my son last week, he became silently wistful and said, "I wish it would snow." This, of course, made us laugh and relay memorable past snow stories. He has spent one Christmas with family in London where it did not snow until the New Year, but has experienced snow many times when travelling in Europe. Looking at my Christmas cards, snow is there in abundance. It is so Northern Hemisphere. I think snow is in my son's acquired consciousness. I remember so many wonderful snow events: sitting by snow-covered stone lions whilst listening to church bells, walking through Hyde Park in the early hours, snow up to our knees.

In all the depictions of the actual Christmas event, there is never snow surrounding the manger, where Mary, Joseph and the baby Jesus are shown. There may be animals, wise men and shepherds, but never snow. Therefore, snow is just one of the many trappings of Christmas, which we love and continue to bring to this event. Some, like the green and red wreaths and flowers are old traditions. Others, like the baubles and fairies on trees are relatively new.

But what does Christmas mean to me? I must admit that now I just attend and go through the motions of presents and celebrations, and long for the time it will be over. I do enjoy seeing the children delight in all the decorations, the trees and Santa that my son and daughter continue to celebrate, but in my own home, I have none of the trappings. Each year, I withdraw more and more from this noisy commercial cardboard ritual.

This sounds somewhat sad, but I shall, as usual, listen to Her Majesty Queen Elizabeth II's speech, watch the service from St. George's Cathedral, or Westminster Abbey, listen to carols and play my CD of the Messiah. This seems to suggest that I am an Anglican or "religious." Not so, but these are the stuff of what Christmas means to me. It is a sense of linking to the past, of the smell of tangerines, the taste of mince pies and the cracking open of nuts. It is of each Christmas bringing a sense of renewal much more so than that of fireworks on the 31st.

This linkage to the past is, for me, all encompassing. Together with a growing reluctance to participate in the pressure of today's conventions, I see the Christian aspect of Christmas diminishing whilst other religions in Australia seem to flourish. Schools are banning nativity displays and carols, particularly those that reinforce Christian traditions.

It is a process which grows, and it is one that shuns and wants to eliminate the basis of a culture founded on Judeo/Christian history and events. As a Humanist, it is the last thing I would want to see destroyed. I would wish that Christian carols continue to be sung (although like Tim Minchin I have trouble with some of the lyrics☺), that the bells continue to be rung, that people shake hands in churches that are not divided by gender, and that the image of a young baby will always signify renewal and goodness.

Frances Richardson

As the Years Go By

New Year's Day, 2013:

Another year over, Meryl Doyle observed as she lifted the previous year's calendar from its hook above the wall phone. Time for another New Year's Resolution. Carefully she placed the new calendar on the hook, and then stood staring at the date. Why bother? she thought, her head throbbing too viciously to utter the words aloud. For the past three years her resolutions had been the same: to move onwards and upwards from this shoebox of a rented apartment. Nothing had changed yet.

Then she wondered if *not* making a New Year's Resolution was like a double-negative, making it one? Thinking about it made her head spin. Clasping her hands against her skull in a vain effort to dull the pain, she considered coffee, but just as she decided to return to bed without her usual caffeine kick, the phone rang.

Meryl moaned as she picked up the handpiece and raised it gingerly to her ear. 'Hello?' she said softly.

The caller, oblivious to her mood, shouting exuberantly, 'I'm going to have a baby!'

Meryl jerked her head away from the phone, recognising the voice of her younger sister, Helen, who obviously did not share her pounding, hung-over head.

When Meryl remained silent, Helen went on, 'Merri? You still there?'

Meryl returned the phone to her ear. 'Yes, I'm still here. Do you mind turning the volume down? Right down.'

'Have a hard night?'

'A long night.'

'You've only got yourself to blame.'

'Thanks for the sympathy. Not!' Meryl heard a cog in her fuzzy brain give an almost audible click. 'Hang on, Hel! What's this about a baby? It's New Year's Day. You don't even have a steady boyfriend. What gives?'

Meryl winced at Helen's laugh down the line. 'It actually hasn't happened yet.'

'Then why are you telling me?'

'Because it's going to happen!'

Meryl wondered what planet her sister had landed on this year. 'Go on.'

'At the buck's party we gate-crashed last night ...'

'*You* gate-crashed,' Meryl corrected, recalling the rowdy group crowding the bar at *The Cut* Golf Club.

Ignoring her, Helen continued, 'A palm reader was there and she offered to read my hand.'

'Of course.' Meryl's sarcasm completely missed its mark.

'She said I will definitely be having a baby this year.'

'Bully for you. May I suggest you go find someone to jump into bed with to make it happen, and allow me to die in peace here?'

'I've found him already. I'm phoning from his bed! His name's Tyler.'

'Am I supposed to cheer?'

'Was the party that bad after we split?'

'Worse.'

'Want to tell me?'

'No.'

'Okay. See you tonight at Mum and Dad's then.'

'You're going to tell *them?*'

'Not likely! You know what dad thinks of Bogans!' Helen laughed again and despite her pounding head, Meryl's lips stretched in a small smile. Helen continued, 'I'm not telling them, Tyler is!'

'Really.'

'He stood beside me the whole reading and listened to every word. I was so surprised he didn't laugh in her face, but he told me later she was his sister.'

'How convenient.' Meryl rolled her eyes.

Finally her sister picked up on her mood and ended the call. Meryl returned to bed and assumed that would be the end of her sister's nonsense.

New Year's Day 2014:

Woken at 5 am, Meryl paced the carpet trying to calm her fractious niece. Once more living with her parents, her life had gone backwards: no job, no flat, and legal guardianship of her sister's baby until Gayle reached eighteen years of age. Her parents had declined the responsibility, citing their advancing age.

The palm reader had been spot-on. Nine months after the phone call, Helen gave birth to a baby girl. What the palm reader did not foresee was the car crash on the way home from the hospital after Tyler celebrated fatherhood far too enthusiastically. Only the three-day-old baby survived.

Meryl was flabbergasted by the discrimination she often encountered as a single woman with a baby; had given up trying to explain it was her dead sister's child. But it was impossible to be angry with the little bundle of new life. A parting gift from her sister, the hospital psychologist said, and Meryl embraced this explanation. Little Gayle was not responsible for her predicament and Meryl was already loving her like a mother, despite feeling so tired she could scream.

Suddenly Gayle emitted a huge burp. 'Good girl,' Meryl crooned. Soon the baby was asleep. Meryl placed her gently in her cot and flopped onto her own bed nearby.

She was not aware of sleeping until her father's voice woke her. 'We're going to the park. Want to come?'

Meryl glanced at the cot. Empty. Her heart froze. 'Where's Gayle?'

'With your mother. You looked so tired we let you sleep when we heard Gayle wake again.'

'Thanks, it was a tough night.'

'Are you coming? It's a lovely day outside.'

Meryl nodded. 'Give me five minutes to get dressed.'

Half an hour later the small family was settled on a picnic rug under a shady tree in a nearby park. The sun was shining without its usual summer sting, leaving the air pleasantly warm. Other family groups were scattered around the park, and in the expansive grassy middle a cricket game was in progress.

Suddenly the ball sailed through the air, heading directly towards the baby cooing and kicking her legs happily in her bouncinette. Meryl tried to scramble to her feet to catch it, but a stranger was more agile.

'Sorry about that,' he said cheerfully as he tossed the ball back.

Meryl squinted up at him, trying to decide if his apology was genuine.

'Hey, haven't I seen you somewhere?' he said to her.

He was standing directly in the sun and she couldn't see him properly. A shout from the cricket players drew his attention and he loped away.

A few minutes later he was back. 'I know where I've seen you before. It was at Tyler Taylor's funeral a few months back!'

Meryl recognised the name. 'My not-quite brother-in-law. How did you know him?'

'He was my younger brother's best mate. That accident fair shook everyone up, I can tell you.'

'Shocked us, too. I still miss my sister.'

'So that's how you're related.' He looked at Gayle now happily playing with her fingers. 'And this must be Tyler's tadpole?'

Meryl squinted at him. The sun was still behind his head and she wished she could see his face properly. 'Yes.'

'Right noble of you to take her on.'

Meryl smiled tiredly. 'Someone had to. Mum and Dad felt they'd be too old by the time she's twenty-one.'

A shout came from the other players but he ignored them. Instead he leaned over and held out his hand. 'Anyway, I'm Hilton Stockwell.'

'Meryl Doyle,' she said solemnly, 'And my parents, Alison and Malcolm Doyle.'

'Pleased to meet you all,' he said pleasantly, shaking hands all round. 'And especially pleased to see Tyler's kid in such good hands.' He squatted in front of Gayle and added his index finger to the toys she was playing with.

At last Meryl could see his face clearly. Open, clear, honest. She liked it instantly.

Meryl's father said, 'What's your opinion of the Taylor family?'

Meryl watched several emotions flicker across Hilton's face as he considered his reply. 'His parents are decent people, but Tyler was a wild child. I'm not sure if he led my brother on or it was the other way round.'

'And what about you?' demanded Malcolm Doyle.

'I admit it, I ran wild for a time too. I've changed now, not touched a drop since the accident.'

'I thought you said he was your brother's mate,' said Meryl, confused.

'Yes, but we kicked around in the same group.'

Another shout came from the players on the grass. 'Coming!' he yelled. Turning to Meryl he said, 'Gotta go, but I need an excuse to duck out of a boozy party tonight. Can I take you to dinner instead?'

Meryl looked at her parents.

'It's time you went out, we can look after Gayle,' said her father.

At more yells, Hilton rose to his feet. 'Call me,' he said, pulling out his wallet, extracting a business card and handing it to her in one fluid movement. He was gone before she could reply.

She studied the card. His name was embossed in gold lettering. I'll Google him before I call, she decided as Gayle demonstrated she'd had enough of self-amusement by starting to cry.

New Year's Day, 2015:

Meryl strolled through the patio checking the decorations and table settings one more time. Lunch for fifty, and only the marriage celebrant and her parents knew it was not to celebrate another new year but a marriage. Hers and Hilton's. Already the biggest diamond she'd ever seen was gracing the fourth finger on her left hand. Meryl smiled, recalling her disbelief when she'd Googled his name and discovered he was a marketing guru for the Bogan movement and one of the most eligible bachelors in Perth.

In a few hours this three-storey mansion overlooking the ocean at North Cottesloe would be her home. Already they'd redecorated one of the ten bedrooms for Gayle, who was now walking and already calling Hilton, "Dada". He had been present when she'd taken her first step. That was when he'd proposed – in his way. Wrapping her and Gayle in a bear hug, he'd said, 'Gayle needs a brother or sister to play with.'

Meryl had tilted her head at him. 'Meaning?'

'Let's give her one.' As Meryl started to protest he added quickly, 'A ring first, we'll make it legal.'

'I suppose that's the closest I'll get to a proposal?' she guessed.

'Yep. I am a Bogan, after all.'

'I guess I could live with that.' They'd kissed until Gayle began wriggling in protest. It had been Meryl's idea to surprise his extended family with the wedding, and New Year's Day the perfect cover.

She made her way to the guest bedroom, where a white lacy dress and veil awaited; reflecting on how much had changed since she'd stopped making New Year's Resolutions.

Shirley Rowland

Santa's Secret

I had the privilege of meeting and getting to know a real Santa. Growing up I dreaded being dragged along by my parents to pose with the snowy white bearded figure in the red outfit, long black boots and white gloves. The figure was trying to be friendly, inviting me to sit next to it and smile at a camera while he asked if I had been good. I pulled away or sat with a frozen half smile, uncomfortable, waiting for the moment I could escape away to my parents.

Christmas holidays usually involved a trip to see this figure while I could never understand why he only seemed interested in me and I had to leave my parents behind as they encouraged me to go and pose with a stranger. It was a horrid experience and if you ever see a photo of me you will see how much I disliked the experience that my parents probably paid for as a treasured memory.

When I got a little older, I realised Santa didn't fly over our house, reindeer bells didn't jingle at midnight on Christmas Eve and those presents didn't appear magically on my bed. Santa became a merry figure appearing on Christmas cards, wrapping paper and tree ornaments. I didn't have to go and have photos taken which was a special treat for children now younger than me.

Many years passed with Santa relegated to one of the icons making an appearance at Christmas or in advertising or Christmas in July lunches.

All that was about to change. I was to have the honour of meeting a real-life Santa.

It didn't happen all at once. The revelation took place slowly over several years.

I got to meet Santa John who was majestic at Christmas when he put on a memorising show for hundreds of children and their parents during the holidays. He was most particular about his appearance and had professionally sworn to uphold all traditions according to the North Pole Santa.

He had shiny long black boots. His beard was extra snowy white with soft curls. His suit clean, crisp and deep red with black belt and white gloves.

His eyes sparkled with warmth and kindness and showed a deep connection with the spirit of Christmas. He loved listening to and talking with all the children who came to see him. He was popular with many shopping centres that would request his presence each year and he had a busy schedule.

Many times, he appeared on the front page of the local community newspapers and he would volunteer at many charity events and worked tirelessly as Santa for many good causes.

He made sure there were enough give away toys for all the children and welcomed everyone of all ages and backgrounds.

He had a childlike love of some foods including ice cream, chips and his favourite Jaffa biscuits. A visit to his rose garden was like visiting a Christmas wonderland. Roses of every colour including ruby red, bright white, dreamy yellow and delicate pink decorated his tidy garden and seemed to bloom extra especially tall with amazing perfumes. These flowers thrived under his love and attention.

We think Santa lives forever and in some way this is true.

A day came when Santa John decided not to appear at Christmas. This came a few months after he was diagnosed with an aggressive form of cancer. Although he dearly loved his role, he didn't want any child to see Santa ill. This would be against the age-old tradition of the jovial fellow with the hearty ho ho ho. That year there was a piece of Christmas missing from their local community.

At the funeral many elves, reindeer and other magical creatures made their appearance. Although dressed in ordinary human clothes, they remembered and recounted lovingly the special times they had shared with their Santa.

His wife, children, grandchildren and great grandchildren and friends mourned a life well lived and a man well loved.

To me Santa is more than a suit, a cheery card, wrapping paper and a shopping centre icon. I was lucky to know a real human Santa who lived and shared with everyone the true spirit of Christmas.

Stephanie Slanzi

Christmas

Until we came to Australia in 1941 the family Christmases had been spent in cool or cold weather climates. Our first six Australian Christmases were spent in Geelong, Victoria where we had settled for the duration of the war. The intention had been to go back to the UK, but the war went on too long. When it ended and our father had retired from his post in India, he joined us in Geelong. He later moved the family to Tasmania where he bought a practice as he wanted to work for himself rather than a government.

The very first Christmas in Australia was in a rented house in Aberdeen Street. The kitchen had a temperamental gas stove, a fly-wire meat-safe and an ice chest. My mother coped as best she could. For a while she attended an evening class in basic cookery at the local Technical Institute as she had never had to cook before. All her married life till then had been spent in India and in what is now Pakistan where employing servants was the normal thing to do and what was expected of the British living there. At the end of the year she brought home an iced Christmas cake she had made, which had a decoration of a Christmas tree on it.

That first Christmas: that is Christmas Day 1941, must have come close to the weekend because Mother suddenly realised that all the shops were closing for four days. By my calculations it was on Thursday which meant the Boxing Day holiday was on Friday and most of the shops would stay closed for Saturday and Sunday She was able to buy a cooked chicken at the delicatessen nearby on Saturday and hoped that would see us through the rest of the weekend until the shops opened again. If we'd had a proper refrigerator it probably would have lasted, but it was a particularly hot weekend and there was only the ice-chest, with the rapidly melting block of ice, in which to keep things cool.

On Sunday the lunch was to be cold chicken and vegetables followed by the remains of the Christmas pudding. Our little brother, aged nearly four at the time, looked at his piece of chicken and said, "there is something wriggling on mine." It had become fly-blown. Mother was devastated. I don't know what we ended up having for lunch, but we did not eat the chicken.

By the next Christmas we had moved to another suburb and a newer rented house which had a modern kitchen. There was a Regulo oven with the gas rings beside it and a big modern refrigerator. There was plenty of cupboard space and the work tops all had inlaid linoleum on them. The Regulo oven had come with its own cookery book so life was a lot easier for our mother after the temperamental gas stove of the previous house. The cookery book included whole dinner menus that could be cooked at the same time using the varying temperatures at the different levels in the oven. Mother would try these out as a gas saving exercise.

I remember the summers as being always hot with the north wind blowing. There was no air conditioning and we didn't even have a fan. On hot days, following an Indian practice our mother, by substituting a wet blanket for the wet reed blinds used there in the tropics, hung the blanket on the fly wire door at the entrance to the house and we played or read in the coolness thus created.

On hot days such as this the tar on the pavement used to bubble. I remember going barefoot to post a letter. The pillar box was at the end of the block. Going was all right but coming back my feet began to feel the heat as I hopped from shade to shade. There were trees lining the street but there were big gaps between them. I ended with some nasty blisters on my feet. We no longer had to suffer the hot north winds of Victorian summers when we moved to Tasmania after the war. It was a much cooler climate and Christmas Day was generally enjoyed in a more pleasant temperature.

Our Christmases followed a usual pattern with filled stockings to start with which we opened together and then gave each other our individual presents. During the morning there was the Church service to attend, followed by dinner with the traditional plum pudding. The bulk of the presents, such as those from overseas, were distributed later at afternoon-tea time. It was not till later, when I had gone to work in England for a couple of years and had spent Christmas with my aunts and their families that I realised what our mother had been trying to recreate.

When Tony and I married, we first lived in central NSW in a place that was bitterly cold in winter and very hot in summer. Our first Christmas there though was quite cool and surprisingly it rained. With a baby, just three-weeks old, I had to light the fire so I could dry the nappies!

We moved to the West and our family increased to four. While the children were still young, we followed our usual pattern. Then stockings were finally abandoned. My mother gave up when it cost more than 10/- to fill them. I gave up when they cost more than $10.00. I wonder how much it would cost now to fill them with the same sort of things. Even the cheapest paperback book costs over $12.00.

As the children became more grown-up, we also changed the pattern on Christmas Day by going, with a festive picnic lunch, to the beach at Cosy Corner after the morning church service. We encouraged some friends to join us there too and for several years we would have a most enjoyable day.

The changing face of Christmas day: families grow up and move away. We have not been to the beach for a long time now. Sometimes we spend a few days over Christmas at Busselton or Perth with one of our children and their family. Sometimes a family will come to us staying in holiday accommodation nearby. The grandchildren are growing up and moving from their homes to their own places. When we were on the farm and the grandchildren were young, we could put up two families and the other family living in the township would come for the day. Now we have down-sized and are living in a small house in the town with only room for one guest. Once we could sit twelve at the big table in the dining room; now it is a squeeze to fit five in the small eating area. Even the Christmas tree was downsized to a very small, artificial one. There is no room for a cut down pine tree any more. At least there are fewer decorations to put away which is something to be thankful for.

Alison P. Smith

Holiday Memoir

We four prospective dietitians were from the Eastern states. In 1955 we had come to complete our qualifications with a one-year graduate certificate course at RPH. In July of that year we had a fortnight's holiday. Jo had flown home to Victoria but for Jen, Maggie and me home was too far away and an airfare too expensive for the short time we had. What would we three do for the fortnight? Miss Wynn, the secretary of the department, had a friend, Christine, living near Albany. Christine and her mother owned holiday cottages at Emu Point outside Albany and leased them cheaply in the off-season. What could be a more *off* than the south coast in midwinter? Miss Wynn said she could probably get a good deal for us if that was what we would like to do. We had seen very little of Western Australia. The furthest south we had been was Bunbury when we managed to get some time off duty together and spent a couple of days there. A holiday in Albany seemed a good idea.

There was a regular overnight passenger train service to Albany which we caught. We could have booked a sleeper, but it was too expensive. At that time our pay as students was minimal. The train rattled down the narrow 3'6" gauge line on its long slow journey southward, stopping with a crunching metallic sound at each station. The driver enjoyed hooting loudly at every road crossing too. We eventually arrived at the Albany railway station after a somewhat cold and sleepless night. The chilly early morning made us thankful for the warm clothes we were travelling in and had also brought with us.

The holiday cottages were a few kilometres eastward along the coast from Albany. We had thought about hitch-hiking, but at that hour trying to hitch-hike did not seem such a good idea. We also had a fair amount of luggage with us for the fortnight. When a taxi appeared, we considered taking it. The driver said he would toss us for the fare "double or nothing", but we decided not to gamble and agreed to pay the proper amount. Emu Point, where the cottages were situated, was then a small seaside settlement. It is now a sprawling suburb of smart houses. We were driven along the narrow road, and the glimpses of sea were soon transformed into a sweeping view of King George Sound with Michaelmas Island and Breaksea Island in the distance.

We met Christine and her mother, the owners of the property. They had bought a Nissan hut from the airport when the American base there was closed at the end of the war. The hut had been cut up into small self-contained units and were established in the bush setting of the property. They had also bought the two-storied tower which they themselves then lived in. We had been given two cottages near each other so used one for sleeping and the other for living.

We had a wonderful holiday there. Though it was mid-winter and chilly I do not remember the weather stopping us from doing anything. I have a photo of us with our bathers and towels outside one of the cottages. The beach was just over the sand dunes, so we were close to the sea and not far from the more sheltered waters of Oyster Harbour. Though it was cold, we swam several times.

Christine was so helpful in arranging for her friends and acquaintances to take us to different places. The owner of the caravan park, Mr Sexton, took us to the Whaling Station near Frenchman's Bay on the other side of Princess Royal Harbour. The Whaling Station was in full production then. The smell was terrible. We stood on the decking watching a whale being cut up. It was all rather gory, but also an education. Dave, the flenser, explained what he was doing. None of us had really thought about the whaling industry before. As we were leaving to find somewhere to have our sausage-sizzle lunch we were given a whale steak to cook for our tea that evening. We were told to cook it with plenty of onions. It was edible and not at all fishy. We made a sort of casserole of it with onions and other vegetables and found it tender.

Terry, another acquaintance of Christine's, took us to a small settlement east of Albany where we had a picnic by the sea and boiled the billy. We had heard about Denmark so decided to see if we could hitch-hike there. We walked into Albany and were able to hitch a ride. Our kind driver said he would pick us up later when he had finished his business in Denmark and take us back to Albany. We spent the time exploring along the river. Denmark was a small pretty place and the area along the river on either side was at that time undeveloped. There was over-hanging shrubbery to negotiate and tall trees also grew there. We had noticed the turn off to Mount Barker. It was only a narrow gravel road. We would have liked to have gone there, but decided it might be difficult to get a lift to see that township. Even if we had reached Mount Barker, we still would have had to find our way back to Albany. We accepted our driver's offer and headed back to Albany when he was ready. Little did I know then that in another ten years I would be living in that area between Denmark and Mount Barker and travelling on the road which was finally sealed in the mid-sixties.

One of Christine's friends offered to row us across the narrow channel that separated Oyster Harbour from the Sound. We were able to explore land on the other side and followed a winding track through the bush to Gull Rock Beach. Here we had an invigorating swim. The water was freezing; it seemed to be coming straight from the Antarctic.

When we were not on excursions organised by Christine, we took ourselves off for hikes to explore the area. I have a blurred photo of us on the way to Bayonet Head, one morning. We are negotiating the rough bush which lined the water's edge and fording the small streams. Now of course it is a smart suburb, but then, there was not even a holiday cottage by the water.

On another day we tried fishing off the rocks below Mt Clarence. We had been told if we made some 'burley' and just threw it into the sea the fish would come. Burley was made by digging up small shell fish from the sand and mixing them with bread crumbs. We did this and having made a few good handfuls went off to try our luck. We found a spot on the rocks beyond Middleton Beach and duly threw in bits of 'burley'. We thought we might have at least got a nibble or two but nothing. So much for the fish coming in shoals to feed on the 'burley!

When we had fruitlessly used up all the 'burley', we decided that that was enough so boiled the billy and had our picnic lunch. There was a gun-port nearby which we investigated. The cannon was still in place then, pointing out to sea to repel any foreigners from invading such as the Germans in the First World War or other foreigners even earlier. Finally, we walked round to Middleton Beach. We took turns on the swings in the playground there before trudging back to Emu Point. It had been an enjoyable outing even if we did not bring home any fish for tea. We'd had plenty of fresh air and exercise.

We must have walked to Albany once or twice for stores unavailable at the local shop. At that time there was a good general store, Barnet's on the Terrace. Here one could buy cheese cut to one's liking, also bacon and cold meats. The grocery items were weighed out into paper bags. It reminded me of the general store my mother used to go to on her weekly trip to Launceston when the family first moved to Tasmania. I would watch in fascination as the bacon curled away from the cutter. A wire fixed to a board with a handle at the other end was used to cut the large cheeses into the required amount. Maggie insisted on buying wheatmeal for porridge rather than rolled oats. The porridge took a bit of getting used to, but it was not too bad. The store must have been one of the last of its kind. Self-service and later supermarkets had taken over ten years later. No longer did one get the personal service of that earlier time.

We were lucky with the weather during our stay, though cold, I do not remember it raining. All too soon our holiday was at an end. Christine once again had been helpful. She arranged a lift to Perth for us in the back of someone's utility, thus saving us our train fare. This was the first time any of us had been on a holiday which was not a family one. It was a great success, we thoroughly enjoyed the time and were so glad we had taken up Miss Wynn's suggestion. I have done my best with my memory and looking at the black and white box-brownie photographs; it is a pity my mother never kept my two long letters written about the trip.

Alison P. Smith

Carawatha

Clickety-clack, clickety-clack, I want to go back, I want to go back.

The wheels of the train taunted Nadine. She didn't really want to go back but she was terrified of what lay ahead. The family would probably hate her.

Too thin for her age with long brown hair stiffly plaited, Nadine clutched her small faded suitcase. Matron had found the time to tie ribbons around the plaits this morning.

'A nice touch of colour for you, child.' The woman spoke kindly. Nadine wondered where Matron had found the ribbons. They were holly green.

'A good Christmas colour,' Matron said. Nadine hoped the ribbons might give her courage.

The battered suitcase held Nadine's few scant belongings: changes of underclothing, her 'good' frock, her mackintosh, a nightgown, slippers and her sponge bag. Nobody at the Children's Home owned very much. Everything was donated and there was never quite enough. Children grew so fast.

Suburban Sydney had been left behind and the train was huffing up the incline of the Blue Mountains. The last stop had been Penrith and now the unfamiliar but strangely exciting names slid by her window: Emu Plains, Glenbrook, Springwood, Lawson, Wentworth Falls and Leura. Wasn't Lawson someone in her school history book?

Trembling fingers clutched at the single 'non-essential' item she owned. Around her neck hung a finely wrought gold chain. Mr

Frantz wanted to take it away from her. He was one of the trustees of the Home, the one who always talked about cost. He said orphaned children were expensive to house, feed and clothe. They shouldn't have 'non-essentials' like expensive jewellery. The chain should be sold to help with her keep.

Matron and Mrs Culverhouse – some people said she was an Honourable, whatever that meant – were very angry with Mr Frantz. Nadine had arrived at the Home with the golden chain: it was hers.

'And you make sure you keep that pretty chain around your neck at all times, dearie,' advised Matron, directing a scowl at the departing Mr Frantz. 'Steal the milk from a baby's mouth, he would. I'll get him off the Board if it's the last thing I do in this vale of tears!'

The train slowed down as it slid towards a station. Mount Victoria. She had been told to get off here. People would be waiting for her. She wondered why this family had asked her to stay for the Christmas holidays, all seven weeks of them. She recalled Matron's words:

'Lovey, some people try to help others along when they can. This year twenty country families asked a Home child to stay for Christmas. It's one of the things Mrs Culverhouse helps organise. She's good at that sort of thing, I'll give her that.'

'They can't really want me. They don't know me.'

'Don't you want to go, then?'

The trouble was she did want to go. She hated the middle of Sydney in the summer. It was hot, gritty and smelly. Being Christmas only made it worse. Christmas was meant to be beautiful. Christmas was for families. She had no family.

'Shouldn't you be gettin' off here, Miss?' The big burly conductor smiled down on her. 'It also happens to be the end of the line for this run.'

She smiled back. She liked his blue peaked cap and smart uniform.

'I think someone's waitin' for you outside, Miss.' He picked up the battered suitcase as if it were a precious burden belonging to an Honourable lady. Nadine crammed her fawn felt hat on her head. She had been sitting on it.

'Here she is, Mrs Cronin, all safe and sound.'

The lady was tall, tanned and wore green slacks with a checked shirt. A wide-brimmed felt hat sat rakishly on short brown curls. The blue eyes were the kindest Nadine had ever seen.

'Welcome, Nadine, welcome.'

Nadine held out her shaking hand, remembered what she had been told to say:

'It is very good of you to invite me and I'll try not to be any trouble. I can make myself very useful around the house and would like to help. I can do just about anything.'

As Marion Cronin later told her spouse, she was stricken with raw fury alternating with a desire to burst into tears. She settled for neither.

'Come and meet Hugh and Snowy.' Marion took the suitcase from the conductor. 'Thanks for looking out for her, Bruce.'

Railway stations seemed much simpler in the country. You just walked past a black iron gate and you were through. And outside –

'Mrs Cronin! Do look, please! It's a horse!'

'That's Snowy. He's a Welsh cob.'

'Do you know him?'

A friendly chuckle was followed by the sudden appearance of a young man. He had been kneeling down on the far side of the horse doing something with its feet.

'And this is Hugh, my eldest son. Yes, Snowy's been part of the family for many years now.'

Nadine shook hands politely with the sunburned giant who had the same kindly smile as his mother but her eyes were for Snowy.

'Want to make friends with him?'

'W-w-w-ould he l-let me?'

'Here.' Hugh dug in a pocket of his moleskin strides and produced a handful of small white cubes.

'Is that sugar?'

'Nope. Salt. Hold them on the palm of your hand and keep your fingers together and still. That's it.'

A tremulous hand gently patted the silken neck. Snowy turned his head, looked at this latest admirer through huge brown eyes fringed by sweeping silver lashes.

'He's a fairy tale horse!' The words burst from Nadine.

'Not in behaviour, I'm afraid,' said Marion Cronin ruefully. 'We've all spoilt him rotten.'

'Is that a cart he's sort of tied to?'

'A trap,' explained Hugh, slinging the suitcase into the afore mentioned vehicle.

'Are we all going to ride in the trap? With Snowy pulling us?'

'Sure are. The fellow's gotta earn his oats.' Hugh grinned at Nadine. 'Mum, just hold Snowy while I help Nadine up.'

Hugh lightly swung the girl up, horrified at the featherweight of her thin body. There was nothing to her. Mentally he frowned: something must be done about that. Marion Cronin joined Nadine and took the reins from her son.

'Not that it's necessary,' she explained, 'Snowy would stand all day given the chance.

After a final check of the errant hoof, Hugh deftly leapt aboard, settled himself and took the reins back.

Snowy walked smartly out of the station yard. Nadine noticed that waves and friendly greetings came from all directions. Snowy sprang into a working trot, his powerful legs eating up the miles. The drive to the farm passed in a dream for Nadine.

Nadine sat in the comfortable stock saddle and patted Snowy. She had been at Carawatha for ten days and Snowy had become a regular part of this wonderful new life. Hugh gave her a few basic lessons and wisely told her to practise what she had learned in the big yard. Her muscles would gradually become used to the unaccustomed exercise then he would take her out to explore the property. The soft mountain air was giving colour to the cheeks that were not quite as thin as formerly and the brown eyes were growing alert and interested. But she still tired very easily and Marion had sternly warned her lively brood not to overwhelm their visitor with too much strenuous activity too quickly. Carefully Nadine collected the reins and made yet another attempt at posting to the trot. A smile lit up her face.

The morning after her arrival Nadine asked to speak to Marion in private.

'In my room, please, Mrs Cronin' she pleaded, biting her lip anxiously.

With the door safely closed, Nadine pulled her suitcase out from under the bed and opened it. Without a word she revealed the contents: all her worldly possessions. Item by item the garments were laid across the bed: the darned and faded undergarments, the shabby fawn mackintosh that was much too large, the neatly patched skirt, the single pair of black lace-up shoes.

'I've just got my 'best' dress and the skirt and blouse I wore to travel. We wear our school uniforms most of the time. We usually get a new dress or jumper for Christmas at the Home.'

Rage bubbled within Marion like hot oil spitting on the stove. Of course! Her own four girls had welcomed the newcomer with delighted enthusiasm: all had been wearing their usual summer garb of shorts and summer shirts with elastic sided boots. Inwardly cursing herself, Marion was careful to remain matter-of-fact.

'Your own clothes are very nice but not quite suited to country living. If you don't mind wearing some of Lucy's things, shorts and jeans would be easier for you while you're with us.' She added with a smile, 'and horses aren't too keen on dresses and skirts, at least, most of them aren't. I know Hugh and the girls are very much wanting to teach you to ride – only if you would like it, of course.'

'Me? Learn to ride? Me? Really?' All thought of the clothing was forgotten.

'Yes, you. I believe Hugh and Lucy have gone to bring Snowy in for you and Sally's checking out a good saddle. What say we go and look out those jeans?'

As Marion made to rise from the bed a spare hand was slipped confidingly into her own.

Nadine – now called Dina – was beginning to love the wild beauty of the Blue Mountains: the contrast of the rugged sandstone cliffs, the eucalyptus forests and the panoramic waterfalls. Every afternoon she would take a book and settle under one of the pine trees. The resinous smell of the pines tickled her nostrils and gentle sleep would gradually claim her. Carawatha was the aboriginal word for place of pine trees. The Kingdom of Heaven that Rector Brown spoke about in Sunday School must be like Carawatha.

Christmas Eve brought the midnight service in the old sandstone church at Mount Victoria. All the family went, driving in what Hugh called a brake. Hugh's Dad drove the spirited matched bay geldings while the passengers sat facing each other on the two long seats which ran along the sides.

The church was lit by candles. The family took up two pews. Nadine, sitting between Sally and Marion Cronin, touched her frock with fingers of wonder. This couldn't be happening to her.

'An early Christmas present,' said Marion earlier in the evening as she deftly slipped the simple blue pinafore frock over the girl's head. It was worn over a white blouse trimmed with real lace. Even the old black shoes looked nice, cleaned and polished to within an inch of their lives.

The choir sang a hymn she had never heard before. It made her want to cry. There had been a time when Mary and Joseph hadn't been welcomed. She wondered if they ever found their own Carawatha.

'Now, Joseph and his wife, Mary
Come to Bethlehem that night,
They found no place to bear her Child
Not a single room was in sight.

Hark, now hear! The angels sing
A new king born today,
And man will live for evermore
Because of Christmas day.'

It was the last week in January when the city lady in the smart suit and gloves left her motor at the front gate. She always enjoyed the walk up the shaded lane.

'Cousin Sarah!' Marion greeted her anxiously.

Slowly the lady peeled away her suede driving gloves and smiled. 'It's going to be all right.' She withdrew two official-looking envelopes from her handbag.

'Fostering for now with the wheels already turning for adoption.'

'Cousin Sarah!'

The Honourable Mrs Colin Culverhouse gave a small wicked chuckle.

'Colin isn't the best barrister in the state for no reason! Why do you think I sent the poor child to you?'

Ingrid M. Smith

Recession Holiday

(In memory of my Dad)

The three of us stared at each other in bemusement.

'You are old enough to understand,' Mother continued, 'that the recession has hit lots of folks. With no steady work for wages for almost a year, we have very little money. Now that school is finished, all of you will have to try to find some way of helping out.'

Our Dad was a builder. He built just about anything you could think of and that included the huge concrete water tanks needed in an area that had never even heard of laid-in water schemes. Rain fell from the sky – sometimes – and ran from the long strips of guttering down into those tanks that were Dad's speciality. Thomsen Tanks, they were called in the shire. Dad was a grand builder – everyone said so but it seemed that people didn't want to build things when recessions came around.

Mother smiled at us understandingly. 'Cheer up! Put on your thinking caps and see what you can come up with. Just do the best you can – no-one expects miracles. Don't forget your afternoon chores. The chicken mash is in the kitchen, Polly.'

I followed Mother through the long plastic strips into the kitchen. I loved our kitchen – it was the best place in our home. It smelt of baking bread, stockpot – which Mum always kept gently simmering on the back of our Aga – chicken mash and cloves. I helped Mum make clove-studded oranges called pomanders. They swung gently from the hooks in the ceiling beams.

'Polly, tell Tommy I need more wood for the Aga, love.'

When I got back outside with the warm bowl of mash, the boys had their heads together.

'– are going to Sydney.' Neil spoke gloomily, kicking a rock with a scuffed boot.

'That's 'cos their nana and pop live there,' reminded Tommy.

'Is Dad on the *pension?*'

'No idea.'

'Dad *couldn't* be on the *pension!* It's for bludgers!'

Tommy cuffed him roundly. 'Cut it out! Don't talk about what you don't understand.'

'Billy Evans says only bludgers get the pension!'

'Say that word again and I'll belt the hide off you!'

It was Tommy who first found a new way to help. Every morning Tommy would take the wooden hand cart out to the native bush two miles from the village. Our Dad had cleverly created the cart from a pair of old-fashioned baby carriage wheels plus odds and ends of spare timber; the smooth handle had once been a broom handle. When it was full of chopped wood and kindling, Tommy walked the two miles back. The wood was sold or bartered to owners of hungry, wood-gobbling Agas. Folks always have to eat.

While I cared for our flock of chickens I racked my brain to think of what *I* could do. Keeping poultry in a small way can be a bit of a dodgy business, if you wish to sell the eggs. The Egg Marketing Board expects all egg sales to go through them so chook owners are only allowed to keep enough birds to supply eggs for the family – at least, that's how it's supposed to work. Twenty birds is the current limit. We have a lot more than that and most of our eggs are bartered. Mr Valladares has six milking cows and we get our milk from him which is paid for in eggs. Miss Cagle keeps bees and her honey is paid for in eggs. That's how it works in our village.

'Move, you!' I gave Sadie, one of our white Leghorns a push. She gave an indignant squawk and scuttled from the laying box. Six large white eggs lay nestled in the straw.

Controversy broke out over the wooden hand cart.

'I need it for something,' announced Neil one morning.

'You can't have it,' Tommy told him flatly. 'I'm using it nearly all the time.'

'What d'you want it for?' I demanded.

'Something special.' Neil tilted his freckled snub nose in the air.

'Tough luck, chum. No can do.' Tommy pushed the cart towards the yard gate.

'Why do you need it?' I reiterated.

Neil relented. 'For old drink cans.'

'Old drink cans?'

'Yep,' Neil nodded very seriously. 'I talked to Mr Higgins down at the dump. He said he'll pay me for collecting old soft drink and beer cans. Bet I can get more money than Tommy and his silly old wood.'

'That's not a bad idea,' I spoke thoughtfully. 'Tell you what. Why don't we take a look in the old wood shed?'

Neil brightened and we headed for the back corner of our big yard where, under a huge pepper tree, the sturdy old wood shed was home to numerous family discards.

'That's it!' I pointed triumphantly at a large dusty object almost hidden beneath a faded blue tarpaulin and a stack of empty chook laying pellet sacks. 'Give me a hand, lazy-bones!'

'But won't Mum want it again?' asked Neil doubtfully as minutes later the old baby perambulator stood proudly on the grass in front of the wood shed.

'I don't think so,' I spoke gently. 'We can ask her if you're worried. Will it do for your cans?'

My tow-headed brother nodded seriously and grasped the pram's handle in two sturdy hands.

My self-confidence had taken a serious jolt. Both Tommy and Neil whom I regarded as my baby brothers had found new ways to help Mum and Dad, to help us all as a *family.* Family meant everything to us. We learnt very early that each member has to pull his – or her – weight or the unit doesn't function properly as a whole.

Neil, once reassured by Mum that she had no further need of the pram, patiently trudged the district searching for those tin cans which had become so very precious to him. Deep ditches, both sides of the fast-drying-up creek, the grounds of our local pub and garbage bins all were grist for Neil's mill. Walking home one afternoon with the pram loaded up, Neil came face to face with Billy Evans.

'Things must be tough at your place, mate, if you're reduced to this. Old man still bludging, huh!'

Billy Evans was older, taller and bigger than Neil. Neil's chin went in the air and he stood his ground.

'Better than working for the dope boys like your old man,' he spoke quietly.

Above his slick new shirt, Billy Evans' fat face turned angry scarlet but his eyes looked scared. It was quite true and we all knew it. Our tiny and remote village on the edge of the Tasman Sea had long been used for drug running. The stuff was taken off on moonless nights by skilled boatmen who met up with the trawlers in international waters. Those dark nights were the only time Billy Evans' Dad did any work.

The massive form of Mr Higgins was approaching. Billy Evans stared at Neil before turning heel.

'Squawk!' Sadie made her usual protest as I remorselessly pushed her aside. There's one in every flock, a real trouble-bird. She's tops at producing eggs though, and today I found seven in the straw-filled box.

In the second coop, Olivia eyed me lazily from the delicious depths of a dirt bath. She is a very large, Large White Orpington, a pretty bird with soft, thick white feathers and like all her breed, lays nice brown eggs.

The last coop was ruled by Rita, a strikingly lovely copper coloured bird with yellow legs and a small pillar-box red comb. Her beak was copper coloured, too. Rhode Island Reds are beautiful birds with their medley of red, black and brown feathers.

The eggs – brown and white – collected, I got to work scraping the perches. Not my favourite task but at least it gives me lots of time to think. The weeks were slipping past and I *still* hadn't found a new way to help our family. I felt I was letting the side down.

One of my daily jobs is to collect the mail from the village post office. Miss Tyrrell-Thomas runs the post office – it is her kingdom for fifty weeks a year. For the remaining two weeks Mrs Norgate takes over while Miss Tyrrell-Thomas takes her annual holiday.

'Registered letter for you, ducks, as well as the usual.' Miss Tyrell-Thomas handed the small bundle of letters across the tall counter. 'And the Major left these.' *These* consisted of a trio of magazines: *Time*, *National Geographic* and *Back Yard Bird.*

The Major is a good sort. He and Mrs Major live at The Manse, the biggest house in the shire. Once, all the lands in the district belonged to The Manse and tenant farmers worked the soil, tended the animals and grew crops but today the Major rules over a reduced domain of barely twelve hundred acres. He keeps a pedigree dairy herd and most of the milk goes to the cheese factory. Our Mum does all the sewing and mending for Mrs Major.

'Thanks, Miss Tyrrell-Thomas.'

'How's your Dad?' enquired that perpetually curious lady. 'Getting along all right?'

I stiffened slightly before replying. 'He's fine, thanks.'

'Keeping well, is he?'

I nodded and fled, not even stopping to pay my usual homage to Jane, an enormous tabby whose favourite perch is the post office counter. I dreaded these ceaseless questions about Dad but was pleased about *Back Yard Bird*, a top poultry magazine only obtainable by annual subscription which was beyond our family resources. The Major bred poultry aiming to improve certain breeds: he also showed his best birds. I walked home slowly with my nose buried in *Back Yard Bird.*

The telegram came late Tuesday morning. It arrived via Miss Tyrrell-Thomas's nephew Frank and his bicycle.

'Thank you, Frank.' Mum's hand was shaking slightly as she took the pale yellow envelope.

'You're welcome, ma'am.'

'What is it, Mum?' The door was closed and Frank's merry whistle could be heard receding down our front yard. Mum's unsteady fingers tore open the telegram.

'*Home on Friday a.m. bus. Hope you waited Christmas for me. Love Jon.*' I read slowly over Mum's shoulder.

It was the first time I saw tears fall from Mum's eyes. They were soon brushed away and we hugged each other joyfully. Our family would be whole again in less than three full days.

Back in early October Dad had left home in the desperate hunt for work. After six weeks searching he landed a labouring job in the mines of the far west, many hundreds of miles away. It was a case of being in the right place at the right time and he was guaranteed two months solid work if he took no Christmas/New Year nor public holiday during that time. It was a chance to be seized upon with eager hands for who knew when work would come again?

I locked my bedroom door before taking the thick envelope from its hiding place beneath my winter clothes. The cheque for five pounds slid out. It came from *Back Yard Bird* and was accompanied by an offical-looking letter. My series, *The Back Yard Bird on a Budget,* so laboriously penned by wavering kerosene lamp over many late nights, was actually accepted for publication.

I could hear eager voices in the living room – what Gran always called the front parlour – the boys were regaling Dad with all their news. Mum bustled about the kitchen preparing the meal to end all meals – I should be there helping her. For the first time in nearly four months home sounded, felt and smelt right again. How I'd missed the delicious rich scent of Dad's pipe tobacco, the sound of his voice and the security of his presence.

I looked at the cheque in my hand. I had finally found a way to do my bit.

Ingrid M. Smith

Bush Christmas

'Twas the night before Christmas
And all through the house
All the family were stirring
Yes, even the mouse!
Whilst Mum packed the snaggers
And chops for the hamper
And Dad rather wistfully
Hoped for a damper
The kids could only excitedly scamper
For just one more peek
At the bush Christmas tree.

At dawn Christmas morning
The youngsters sprang out
And opened small parcels
Oh! just hear the shout.
Then down to the dam
To unpack food to eat
Or jump in the water
To escape from the heat
Or sneak up on the roos
Whose large jumping feet
Took them off and away
On that bush Christmas day.

And late in the evening
The tired family lay
Whilst Mum read the story
Of that first Christmas day
And there in the cool,
And the darkness on high
Was a heavenly star
That shone bright in the sky.
And the wonder and glory
Brought tears to the eye
As the moon cast her light
On that bush Christmas night.

Molly Smith

Holiday Bliss

As a dairy-farming mum in the 1960's/70's I welcomed school holidays with unconcealed joy. Not only were the youngsters around to be part of the farm activities and special outings, but for two glorious weeks the trauma of having the family ready for the school bus on time, as well as feeding the calves in the dairy, was lessened considerably when the school bus was taken out of the equation.

Picnics and barbecues over an open fire in a favourite rocky area of the paddock, rides on the horse and the tractor and watching for baby lambs and calves were very much a part of the holidays as well as farm chores. Long days of play in the open pastures – often with the addition of young school friends from town who enjoyed the taste of farm life. No such thing as *being bored* on the farm.

Christmas holidays were greeted with even more enthusiasm from me as there were six wonderful weeks of non-school-bus bliss. And let's face it, the older children could even be given some shed duties to ease the load on Mum.

Summer holidays meant trips to the beach and sometimes even a few sleepovers in the little beach hut at Peaceful Bay when Dad could be persuaded to take on the dairy duties alone.

Of course it's only natural that in the long holiday at the end of the year, Christmas day was very much on the minds of the younger members of the family. Even the thought of that special day made their eyes sparkle more than ever and Father Christmas became almost a member of the family.

Our family would have gladly cancelled the milking on Christmas morning but their dad pointed out patiently but firmly that our dairying enterprise not only provided the household with milk but with many other essential home comforts as well, and the cows must be milked.

One could hardly blame the youngsters of course. Hadn't they passed through the lounge room and seen the decorated Christmas tree, the little Nativity Scene prepared lovingly the day before and the floor literally covered with gaily wrapped parcels of intriguing shapes and sizes, their bulges and hollows teasing the probing childish fingers.

But the job had to be done and as he left to bring in the herd, their dad suggested that it would be accomplished much quicker if we had extra help in the dairy. Having issued that challenge he went on his way.

By the time he returned and we were ready to start, four beaming youngsters – clad in a motley array of work clothes and rubber boots (first in, best served) arrived at the shed and thus commenced one of the most efficient and speedy milkings on record.

As each group of cows was brought into the shed, eager hands washed the dirt off the teats and more busy fingers were ready to attach the teat cups. When each cow had given the last drop of milk, the teat cups were whisked off and the group of cows ushered out of the shed. Five of us tripped over each other in a space where two or three at the most usually worked. The youngest was delegated outside to move the cows out of the holding yard quickly, in order that said yard wouldn't be littered with the inevitable deposits which had to be hosed away.

Even the old dairy matrons seemed to have the Christmas spirit. In normal circumstances anything different in the milking routine caused an upset, but they good naturedly accepted the hyperactivity and bustling efficiency and simply lifted an enquiring eyebrow or cocked a questioning ear as they were hustled into and out of the shed without having time to realise they had even been there!

At last the final cow had gone on her way and only the cleaning up needed to be done. Again the extra hands flew into action and the last stage was soon accomplished.

Only then did four pairs of legs carry their excited owners to the house with a brief pause to give the hens and dogs a Christmas drink of milk.

They changed into clothes more suitable for Christmas and faced up to the agonising decision of which parcel to open first – Christmas day had REALLY begun!

Molly Smith

A Day with a Difference!

Something was wrong! She was singing Happy Birthday to him, then her voice disappeared. Now there was nothing; no voice and no dial tone.

"Are you there, Sis? Are you okay?" he queried with concern. Melanie, his sister always rang early to sing Happy Birthday. But her bright cheerful voice had faded, completely gone and he was worried. A quick phone call to his brother-in-law gave him no answers either. Cliff was half way to work and jokingly replied, "Ahh you know what your big sister's like. She'll be pulling your leg once again and has probably hung up on you. Don't worry about it, mate. See you at our place for tea tonight. Oh, by the way, Happy Birthday!"

Tony had chosen to take the day off work; a day of rest and relaxation was just what he needed to recharge his batteries. What better way to begin the day than with a leisurely walk down to the park and back again before breakfast, even though it was chilly outside.

The weird phone call was soon forgotten, until arriving at Melanie's later in the day.

My eyes lit up as my brother came into the kitchen. I insisted he join everyone else in the lounge.

"I'll be there in 5 minutes. I want to share the unbelievable events that unravelled for me earlier in the day.

Tony's eyebrows arched up as he looked sideways at her with a puzzled expression on his face. Shrugging his shoulders, he did as he was told!

Family conversations stopped when I entered the room; everyone anticipated I would say tea was ready.

"Before we have tea, I want to share something with everyone. This morning I rang Tony to wish him a happy birthday, but then something strange happened."

"I'll say it did," interjected Tony, "One minute you were singing to me and then … … …".

I cut him off mid-sentence. "Listen! Just listen for a minute! This is important. Instead of talking to Tony, all of a sudden I found myself sitting in the middle of a noisy restaurant. I was confused, disorientated and sitting alone at a table with two chairs. Everyone around me spoke in Irish accents that were difficult to understand. I was baffled. How did I get there? One minute I was in Perth and suddenly I was somewhere in Ireland. Eventually, I was able to call over a waiter as he bustled past me. It must have been obvious I was out of place here, but all he did was re-assure me he'd be back with the drinks list and menu shortly. He reminded me I was not the only person waiting for assistance in this busy location! I shrugged my shoulders and sat back to wait."

My thoughts tumbled around in my head like they were in a washing machine, until a deep masculine voice cut into them. He was asking me if it was possible to take a seat at my table. All the other chairs were now taken and there were no spare tables.

I glanced up to see a frail and elderly gentleman leaning heavily on his walking stick. His eyes were a brilliant blue, hair as white as snow and there around his neck was a white dog-collar as worn by Priests. How could I say no. "Oh, of course you can!"

Gently easing his weary body down into the chair, he murmured, "Thank you for your generosity, young lady. My name is Maewyn."

"You're very welcome Maewyn, it's a pleasure to meet you".

I introduced myself and told him I was a 'blow in' and had no idea I was going to be surrounded by this many people.

"It's certainly been a day of surprises so I'm thrilled you chose to sit and talk with me today."

"Ah, yes, it is a little busier than normal," he chuckled.

Tilting my head, I gazed up at him. It felt like my eyebrows joined together as they moved down closer to my eyes.

"I don't want to pry, but are you a priest? I am not a regular church goer, but I'm always keen to listen to those who do attend regularly."

Maewyn smiled and went on to tell me that he was a priest. He was surprised by my interest, because some people ran for the hills when they saw him coming. Others couldn't wait to gather around him; many asked questions while others were happy to just listen.

I was very interested, so I asked him to tell me more about himself, and how he became to be a priest".

He warned me it was a very long story.

My guess was that he was a very good story teller and I did have time to listen.

But I suggested we order a drink and a meal first. Our order was taken and to keep the hunger pains at bay we were soon sipping on a lemon, lime and bitters with our meal arriving soon afterwards; a Sunday Roast for Maewyn and Vegetarian Lasagne for myself.

By consensus, we agreed to enjoy every morsel of the scrumptious food in front of us first. Then Maewyn made himself comfortable and began to tell me his story.

He'd been born in Britain a long time ago and was taken from his village at the age of 16, sold into slavery in Ireland, where he served as a shepherd for six very long years. He became a Christian during that time. One night while asleep he heard a voice telling him to leave and as there was a ship waiting along the coast. Maewyn was amazed as there really was a ship. Eventually he made his way back to family in Britain. His life turned itself around when he chose to study in a Monastery, where he stayed for 12 years. On returning to Ireland he adopted the Christian name Patricius (or Patrick) and was appointed as a Bishop. Travelling throughout the country he established many monasteries, churches and schools. He also converted many Pagans to Christianity. Many times he was also arrested but luckily for him, he was just as successful in escaping.

I asked if he was still working as a priest and he replied, "A Priest maintains his commitment and faith in God forever." Maewyn worked for 30 years, dying on March 17th. But it was many centuries after his death before a local Bishop declared Maewyn be known as Saint Patrick."

Wrinkles creased my forehead, eyebrows arched and with mouth wide open I exclaimed, "Hang on. Are you telling me you're not a real person?" I began to wonder who he really was.

The mysterious man briefly looked down, before gazing into my eyes which were bulging out of their sockets.

To him it didn't matter so he replied, "You can call me whatever you like; a ghost or spirit. He went on to explain that every year on the 17th March, he sat and enjoyed the festivities along with everyone else. By taking the time to sit with someone like me, he had fun educating others who had no idea about the person Saint Patrick or the significance of this important day.

He continued by explaining, originally Saint Patrick's Day was just a Catholic holiday. In the past, often, religious events had to be disguised and seen as an excuse to have food, drink, music, dance and play games! Now in 2019, it is a day of celebration by people all over the world.

There was silence for a short time, as I pondered what I'd heard.

Once my tongue caught up with my brain, I chipped in;

"This is amazing. No-one's going to believe that I have been talking to Saint Patrick."

Then I asked, if it were true he had banished all the snakes out of Ireland?

Now he was highly amused. His eyes twinkled as he replied "There were many legends created about me. No! There were never any snakes on Ireland during my time there. But something I did do was pray when people were starving. My prayers were always answered and food was provided to all those who were hungry."

I was so excited, but somehow, I knew my time was limited and I needed to bombard him with a few more questions while I had the opportunity.

"So, what about the colour green, the shamrock and the leprechaun?"

Maewyn's belly laugh was infectious and tears streamed down his face. Others nearby turned in their seats to investigate what was so funny.

Maewyn was enjoying the inquisition and went on to provide more information.

"Originally it was the colour blue, but slowly over time that changed to green because of the lush countryside that is seen everywhere in Ireland. The colour green also appears on the national flag. The shamrock is the national flower. And you, young lady, will need to use your own imagination to figure out why there is a leprechaun!"

Right at that precise moment I heard a loud continuous beeping sound and my stomach lurched up into my mouth.

I looked around but everyone and everything from Ireland had disappeared. Now, there was nothing except the phone in my hand. I quickly realised you had hung up, Tony, so I called you back, but your phone was turned off! It's been a frustrating day, waiting to share these events with you. I felt like I was in a dream, but at the same time everything was so real.

I know it's your birthday Tony. And people from all over the world have been celebrating Saint Patrick's Day. But somehow I was in Ireland today and I met Saint Patrick.

My brother cautiously glanced over at me before continuing, "That's enough. C'mon Sis, pull the other leg with the bells on it. It's my birthday. I'm starving hungry and I've been waiting all day to celebrate with my family."

I felt the tears well up into my eyes. I wanted to continue but fell silent. Of course, no one was going to believe me. It was definitely *a day with a difference.*

Maxine Spencer

In A Tight Pickle!

"I'm never going to be caught like this again," Katherine grumbled under her breath as she yanked, pulled and pushed the overflowing trolley.

"Last minute Christmas shopping is a nightmare and don't get me started on this damn trolley. It has a mind of its own, wobbling this way and that and now it feels like I'm pushing a semi-trailer up a hill. Never again!".

The scorching hot easterly hit her as she left the air-conditioned shopping centre. Any other day of the year, she would have stayed to enjoy the cool comfort of her favourite café with a cuppa, and the chance to read her book; that was certainly not happening today.

Her head ached, each foot throbbed from repeatedly kicking the trolley, causing her to wince, with pain shooting from lower back into her hips. Limping, and using the trolley as a support, Katherine hobbled back towards her car.

Earlier the carpark had already been bursting at the seams. But luckily a bay had come up quickly and closer than she thought. Looking up, Katherine spied the little car she called Queenie squashed even tighter than before. She was horrified to see that one thoughtless and selfish driver had driven into their bay, while the other had reversed in, both straddling the dividing white lines. This allowed both of those driver's adequate space to exit their own vehicles with ease. However, neither had given any consideration to Katherine or Queenie.

With her brain scrambling into overdrive, she wondered what her options were. She parked her trolley in front of one of the offending vehicles. Breathing in and turning sideways she inched her way down to the driver's side of the vehicle. There was not even the slightest chance of getting either door open more than an inch or two. She shuffled backwards and peered down the other side, once again squeezing her slim body between the two cars. The door opened slightly, but only enough to allow one arm to enter her car.

"How am I ever going to get into you, Queenie? What are we going to do?"

After a moment or two pondering possibilities, "Of course! Through the boot!"

Katherine cringed as she looked at the contents in this hidden compartment; everything, including the kitchen sink, was crammed in there! Bags and boxes for a local charity, things to be repaired or replaced, the 'just in case' sunscreen and mozzie gunk. Why on earth she wondered, did she still have jumper leads, when a phone call to the roadside assistance now solved all motoring issues. Under a ton of other totally useless stuff, Katherine discovered her trusty torch and the deck chair that had both been missing for years. This was all so embarrassing, but now in utter frustration, the whole lot was thrown in a heap near the fully laden trolley.

What a sight! Katherine felt, rather than saw, other people hurry by as she clambered into the boot. She pulled down the strap in the back seat exposing a small hole. Was it going to be big enough? Would she get stuck?

She felt like an idiot when passing children asked embarrassing questions, followed quickly by "Shhhhhhhh, come on, hurry up," from their parents.

Other fleeting comments also 'dug the barb' in even more.

"Oh my goodness, someone's trash is always someone else's treasure. I wonder if there is a pre-Christmas garage sale happening here today."

"Hey, Charlie, take a look at that!" as a wolf whistle rung in the air.

But her perseverance and determination, along with lots of huffing and puffing kept her moving forward. Everything hurt, including her pride as she pushed her tired and sore body to finally collapse in behind the steering wheel.

She could hardly believe her eyes when a glance in the rear-view mirror revealed nothing but the opened boot lid. She knew there was not much space to reverse out into. Rubber necking took on a whole new meaning as she swiveled her head from left to right and back again time and time again as the car inched its way out of the cramped parking position it had been trapped in.

Katherine blocked out the symphony of honking horns along with the cursing and yelling of 'Come on hurry up!' It became an art in itself, as she dodged the many unofficial racing car drivers as they impatiently roared around her as she slowly reversed out.

Feeling like she'd run a marathon, Katherine just wanted to collapse; under the car would do! All that Christmas shopping still needed to be loaded into Queenie, along with everything else that was strewn on the ground. Could she leave it there? She felt tempted. No, not now. Oh, the stress of it all.

With thudding heart, her face almost purple, wet through with perspiration, tears so close, headache pounding, her bladder chose that very moment to raise its ugly head, screaming to be released.

Just as the last few things were relocated back into the boot, Katherine slowly pulled a pen and some paper from her handbag. Two identical notes were scribbled and left under the windscreen wipers of both offending vehicles. So many things could have been written in anger, but weren't.

'To the driver of this vehicle. I forgive you.

Please enjoy and stay safe over the Festive Season'.

In a daze she closed the boot and moved the trolley into her now vacant parking bay.

Opening the driver's door, Katherine was startled at the beeping sound as both monsters beside her were unlocked at the same time.

She stood frozen for what seemed to be an eternity, but no one appeared.

What a blessing as she switched on Queenie's air con and drove out of the crazy car park.

In years to come, Katherine pondered, this could become one of the funniest summer and Christmas memories ever. Belly laughs would erupt as she told the tale of how she tackled and survived being caught *in a tight pickle!*

Maxine Spencer

A Room with a View

The clothes in my small case magically transform into bricks as I drag it down narrow concrete steps into the depths of the Italian train station. The plastic wheels slip from one worn step to the next and threaten to tumble me in a downward spiral to some hidden Roman Hades.

Tired from sitting on the train for what seems like an entire day, it is a relief when the taxi speeds through the narrow streets to the hotel on the outskirts of Stresa. The building has seen better days, and from her rumpled blouse to her cracked leather shoes so too has the manageress. Grey hair escapes the severe bun that drags every bit of femininity from her face.

Without wasting a word of welcome, she thrusts a sheaf of papers at us. By now we are familiar with the mandatory forms demanded by the Italian Government for those fortunate to spend time in the land of Caesar and spaghetti. Once lodged with the nearest police station our every detail will be on record. (Should we try to eat our spaghetti with the aid of a spoon, or demand the meat course before, or even with, the pasta, our ignorance will forever mark as us mad foreigners).

With one hand she grabs the completed forms, and with the other gives us a key. At the same time she points towards a staircase at the side of the gloomy entrance hall. Foolishly we stand and wait for someone to take our cases as she returns to shuffling papers on her desk. With a shrug we snap out the handles and trundle our luggage across the hallway.

The room number, 309, means we must negotiate three flights

of stairs, in complete darkness. Either the lights don't work, or our unhelpful host thinks us unworthy of a single beam from a 60 watt globe. This passageway doesn't just go up – it roams across corridors, the uncarpeted wooden floors echoing with the clacking of wheels.

We reach the door but the key refuses to turn and dumping our cases on the ground we bicker tiredly about who will fetch another key. Before tempers fray any further, I jab at the keyhole one last time and the door opens, dropping us into the room. A disappointing vision of three single beds lined up like cigars in a cheap tin, confronts us, nothing like the image we booked online. A narrow space leads to a balcony beyond.

In single file we sidle past the tiny round table and two metal chairs that occupy most of the flimsy outside ledge. With eyes only for the view, we each let out a contented sigh. Across Lake Maggiore a blue mist rolls from distant mountains towards us over the shimmering waters. The cawing of seagulls fills the air and the fragrant scent of camellias drifts over our travel-jaded souls.

Smiles light up our weary faces; this is why we travel so many thousands of miles, to experience such moments together. High above the lake, as Mother Nature displays her best, not one word passes our lips.

And then we hear the buzzing.

"We must be next to the laundry. That's a washing machine emptying," says one sister, but the other disagrees.

"Maybe there's a fridge against the wall next door," she says.

"No," I say, "it's an insect trapped in the walls."

The prospect of trying to sleep with this irritating insect for company drives me to storm back down the miserable corridors to confront our unfriendly manageress.

Still sitting at the front desk where we left her half an hour ago, she picks chipped nail polish from her blunt nails with a lethal-looking emery board. I try to explain our predicament, but my

Italian is no better than her English and I resort to beckoning and repeating "per favore." Stony-faced, she heaves herself to her feet and clomps ahead of me as we return to room 309.

Pointing to the still-buzzing wall and with arms flying like Quixote's windmill, each one of us try to explain why we want a different room, one without the noise. Her frown grows bigger than any of ours as she points to the balcony with the marvellous lake views and shakes her head.

We decide she means no other room boasts this wonderful balcony, and we are quite 'loco' to want to move. In sisterly harmony we all 'buzz', thinking she misunderstands our reason for leaving this most fortunate of rooms. With a movement quicker than any we have seen her make so far, she walks over to a suitcase beside the wall and mimes turning a key.

My sister heaves her case onto the bed and after unlocking it, throws open the lid. A transparent plastic bag lies on top of her neatly ironed clothes. Inside, the head of a battery-operated toothbrush spins madly around, accompanied by the now much louder buzzing sound.

One by one we fall across the bed, doubled up with hysterical laughter, much to the disgust of our host. With one last look at the three of us, she leaves, closing the door behind her with a slam.

Silence fills the room until someone says, "Buzz, Buzz," and off we go again, clutching our stomachs as we roll around.

The final victory is hers though. After reading the hotel brochure, we talk of dining in their restaurant, famed for its fresh lake fish. But none of us dare show our faces downstairs. Instead, we sit on the balcony and pass around crushed packets of biscuits left over from lunch on the train. Plastic bottles of lukewarm water replace the Italian wine we planned to sample throughout the evening.

But the view of the lake is magnificent.

Wendy Stackhouse

Dear Karen

Dear Karen,

For once I am sorry to say I can't agree with both your and Alex's recommendations for our holiday. The hotel is nothing like you described – it's an old Victorian mansion in need of major repairs.

Early this morning we walked down to the jetty to find our boat missing – the harbour was as deserted as our hotel.

Alex has tried phoning for help and could not get through to anyone. Both his mobile phone and mine have disappeared since we came here, and the landlines in the hotel don't work.

I don't know why you recommended this particular island. Had I not been so busy at work I would have researched the place myself, but you know how frantic things have been. As my executive assistant, you have always had my best interests at heart, but this place is nothing like you described.

From the boat the other morning I noticed a small village on the other side of the island. We intend walking there tomorrow to see if there is a local post office. At least we can use their phone, and find out when the next boat arrives, so we can leave.

I will post this from there, there must be a mail-box of sorts, so I'll sign off now,

Keeping my fingers crossed we'll be home soon!

Cheryl and Alex. XX

*****

Dear Karen,

It's been a few days since my last letter, and nothing has changed!

We walked to the village – a two-hour tramp around the island on roads that are not even wide enough for a car. Although we saw no animals, we saw signs of hoof prints in the dirt road. Near the village, we found a desiccated sheep's skull stuck on a rotting wooden fence.

The village itself showed no signs of life – and looked as if it had been that way for a very long time. We found a post office, but like every other building in the village it was empty. As the door was open, we tried the phones, but they were all as dead as the ones in the hotel. The mailbox outside gaped open – and anyway, what postie would empty a box in a deserted town? So now I will have to keep this letter, along with the first one until we find another mail-box or a boat arrives.

Each morning we go to the jetty, but not so much as a rowing boat has been near the island. I'm sure the sound of anything else, like a helicopter would have woken us up. We are, as you can imagine, not sleeping that well.

Tonight we intend to keep watch over the jetty, it may sound dramatic but we are getting worried. Food is not an issue – the pantry in the kitchen is well stocked. So is the wine cellar, which I am not ashamed to say we have visited frequently. As Alex says, we paid a fortune for this private island retreat and we should at least get our money's worth. We will sleep all afternoon, so we can stay awake for our vigil throughout the night. If any kind of vessel arrives, we will insist they take us off here.

I will keep both these letters with me, in case a boat arrives and can take, if not us, at least our mail, back to the mainland.

Alex is calling me to join him in a glass of Mouton Rothschild, and with a wheel of French Brie and a packet of Raincoast Crisps, we will dine in splendour – albeit isolation!

Hope this reaches you soon, and even better, hand delivered by me!

Love Cheryl and Alex.

*****

Dear Karen,

Another week has slipped by with no sign of boats or other people. Our holiday is over before it even began, and we are no closer to leaving here.

The weather is the only thing this island has going for it. The sun is out every single day, yet the nights remain cool and bearable. We go about the island in shorts and tank tops though by evening we need a light jacket.

The night-time vigils at the jetty proved a waste of time – nothing comes near this place. After a fortnight we have almost given up trying to get off the island. I suggested lighting a signal fire from the top of a nearby hill, but Alex didn't think it was a good idea. He said it was too dangerous, and might set the hillside alight. You know him; he never thinks any of my suggestions worthwhile, and so it did not surprise me. This time though if things don't improve in the next day I will climb up the hill and light one myself. He can stay and drink himself into a stupor, which he has been doing for several nights now.

Even though you are my best friend, I didn't tell you that this holiday was a last-ditch attempt to patch up our marriage. When Alex suggested we get away from everything and give it a last go, I felt I had to agree. For some time now I have wanted us to go our separate ways.

My company, with your able assistance, has been doing well for several years now. Alex on the other hand has driven his company into near bankruptcy. I tried to warn him to slow down on his drinking and be a more hands-on C.E.O but he ignored my advice. Now there is little left to save. His company shares have begun a downward spiral which they can never recover from. In contrast, mine have continued on an upwards trajectory. He throws this back at me when we argue, which we do more and more these days.

When we return, I will get in touch with my lawyers. I need to make sure the pre-nup agreement we made when we married five years ago is air-tight. Alex has shown no change in his attitude or slowed down on his drinking since we arrived. I will go ahead with the divorce I warned him about before we left. I wish I'd never listened to his ridiculous idea of having a break to sort things out.

This all hinges on getting off this god-forsaken island! I am even thinking of slipping these letters into some of the many empty bottles we have accumulated.

Sorry to offload all this on you, Karen, you have been such a good friend for so long now,

Love
Cheryl.

*****

Dear Karen,

After a few more days of watching a drunken Alex stumble around the hotel, I took charge of things. Last night I lit a signal fire and stayed with it most of the night in case it got out of hand. I ran out of wood by morning so today I will gather a larger pile though I will have to do it when Alex is asleep or passed out. He was furious when he found out what I'd been up to all night. I told him if he couldn't help get us out of this place I would, and he slammed the cellar door in my face! He's still inside, but he can stay there for all

I care and drink himself to death – I want to go home!

Food supplies have dwindled, and now we eat from tins. Though the generator continues to provide us with electricity, I don't know how long it will last. I don't have a clue about anything mechanical. Neither does Alex, though I wouldn't ask him anyway, he's not apologised, or even come out of the cellar.

I am on my way down to the jetty after I finish this letter and seal it in a bottle. The other two letters are already inside bottles, with the corks hammered in tight. I can't think of anything else to do, other than the signal fires. I won't be telling Alex about the bottles either, I can do without his mocking.

Believe you me, when I get off this island I never want to leave the mainland again, ever. My travel agent can keep his Greek Islands, Hawaiian Retreats, and Fijian Resorts. Good old Australia is my destination from now on.

Off to find a hammer and another empty bottle – not hard as bottles litter the tables in every room. When I drop the three bottles off the end of the jetty, the afternoon current should send them bobbing along to the mainland. Afterwards I will go down to the cellar and have a long talk with Alex.

Love
Cheryl.

*****

Newspaper Article – Northern Territory News

A man walking his dog on a remote Arnhem Land Beach has made a remarkable discovery. Caught by rocks inside a tide-pool, he found three bottles, each with a message inside. He handed them in to the Northern Territory Police, who had them examined by experts flown in from Darwin. The letters, deemed authentic, have thrown light on the disappearance of Cheryl Costigan. Reported missing by her husband Alex over two years ago, her body has never washed up along the beaches.

According to Mr Costigan, his wife Cheryl disappeared when their boat capsized near the remote island they were to holiday on over two years ago. A mutual friend of the couple, Karen Macclesfield, (now the second Mrs Costigan), alerted the coastguards to the whereabouts of the missing couple when they failed to return from their holiday. According to Mr Costigan's testimony at the time, after he swam to the island he spent several weeks scouring the waters for signs of his wife.

Mr Costigan, and his new wife, Karen, the former executive assistant of the late Mrs Costigan, are now co-owners in his late wife's business. From their luxury mansion in Kings Head the couple made a joint statement. They said the messages in the bottles were nothing but a cruel joke. The contents of the messages, according to our informants, promise to turn this case on its head.

Newspaper Article – Northern Territory News

Police arrested two people today at the home of Mr and Mrs Alex Costigan. The arrest came after the discovery of human remains on the remote island of Adobinga. The remains, identified as those of the missing Mrs Cheryl Costigan, came to light when Detectives acted on information found in the now famous 'Message in the Bottles'.

Police say they have evidence of a plot between the present Mrs Costigan and her husband Alex. They conspired to get rid of the first Mrs Costigan and take over her million-dollar company. Though the couple deny it, emails between the pair, produced as a proof of intent, back up these claims.

Further examination of the skull shows blunt force trauma as a cause of death. Detectives found a hammer alongside the remains, which were stuffed in an empty wine barrel in the cellar.

Lawyers for the millionaire couple continue to give a 'No Comment' reply to our reporters.

Wendy Stackhouse

Birthday Theft

The first twelve months that I lived in England, on a Teacher Exchange programme, I spent every holiday, weekend and individual days, seeing this country on foot. It was the best of times to be in England.

The last local building to be spray cleaned: the Cunnard Building in Liverpool, had come up to reveal the jewel it was intended to be all those years ago.

Farmers were updating their solid, stone barns to thousands of pounds worth of Real Estate or converting them to very nice B & Bs. I walked each and every weekend, and school holidays with Ramblers' groups. I also spent ten days moving across the country, at four miles per hour, in a very basic canal boat. It was the hottest summer in years and I joined the neighbours sitting out on the street kerb as the houses, sealed against the cold, were too hot to be in. All of these positives influenced my decision to stay longer.

During those twelve months I had spent a lot of time looking at the physique, and the facial features, of men hoping to see some resemblance to the man who was making my next move possible. Our maternal grandfather was the one English member of the four grandparents, but he would entitle me to claim an Ancestry visa and stay longer, even up to four years, and to work in Britain.

The second year in England I did what the Brits do: I left the country. I set off for Ireland and to see if I could spot any resemblance to the other three grandparents who had been born in Australia to Irish parents. My sister had been in England and Ireland twelve months before I set off and she had warned me: you won't recognise anybody in England but you will see clones of our children and our cousins in Ireland.

This trip ended up providing me with a series of firsts. At Manchester Airport I saw, for the first time, two SAS soldiers standing, shoulder to shoulder, with their large rifles across their folded arms. I tried to recall what happened in our airport at Perth but could not remember even seeing police there.

Another breathtaking event at that airport was my introduction to body patting for security, and having to remove the very warm, hair hugging hat to disclose the mess underneath it. It was 1996 and was years before the upsurge of worldwide religious terrorism, but the previous year in England had introduced me to the workings of the IRA. Often, as I stood waiting for a train to get to work, an announcement would tell the passengers on the platform that a bomb scare had been received. We would then have to run for a bus. If a bomb exploded it meant the local authorities had not taken the threat seriously. Along with the body search at the airport my passport was scrutinised, I was scrutinised and eventually I was allowed to proceed to the plane and the very short trip across the sea to Ireland and to Dublin.

What on earth would this country, that had their powerful neighbour so fearful, do with me?

No passport check, no body check, nothing! I walked out to the waiting area and saw a clone of my son. Same age, same colouring, same height, and I bit back the call to ask him what he was doing here?

In Dublin I stayed at a B & B for a couple of days and learnt one lesson in how to look after an aged person wanting to stay in their home until they die. This host of the B & B said she would put her friend in a different room almost each day. The best china and cutlery were used. Fresh flowers from the garden were picked and put into the owner's best vases. This woman stayed with her friend until the end and was rewarded with the house and her new career as the owner of the B & B.

For several days I moved among the local people in Dublin and wondered that you could see people speaking the same language, looking the same as those I had spent twelve months with, yet everything about their behaviour was different. In England, where I lived, the couples walked arm in arm, strolling actually, which made my strides hard to adjust to find some space on the footpaths and to walk at my pace These locals crossed the road when the lights turned green.

In Dublin, people would gather at the side of the road and when five or so assembled, they just took off. If you asked them where something was, even in a department store, they would indicate where to go, and then take you, matching stride for stride.

These were the people holding a neighbouring, much larger country to ransom! How? I was to discover how when two methods of their subversive activities were meted out to me.

This was Easter time which, with school holidays, would give me enough time to enjoy this visit. Wrong!

People such as myself, and the Queen, who have birthdays in March or April, are sometimes dogged by the greater celebration of Easter making their birthday seem second rate. Not so the Irish. When I woke up on Easter Sunday; my birthday, they had stolen one whole hour from my life. It was the start of Day Light Saving.

I had booked my accommodation in an apartment, across the country and on the West coast and was to get there by coach. First I needed to eat. I went into a small café/delicatessen and had a ham sandwich and a cup of tea.

On the coach I did see quite a bit of the country and I heard the people speaking in polite and friendly ways, and then I had to extricate my luggage from under the coach, myself.

Things then happened. I needed a toilet, quickly, and the person who was to meet me was not there and soon there was no one near the bus stop. I waited as long as I could on the street, in this small hamlet, and then made my way to another B & B and started to book in. I used their toilet, just in time, and when I came out to do the official signing in a woman claimed me. People in this small hamlet, really just a semi-circle of houses, had witnessed this stranger moving around, and seen where I had gone, they had then passed that information on to the right person.

My Official Greeter arrived and she helped set me up in the correct apartment, to tell me the cake, placed on the table, was for me, and then she left me to myself.

The knowledge that the ham sandwich was just another strategy to make sure visitors knew that Ireland, and its people, were not to be dismissed lightly, had now hit home. I spent two days running back and forth to the toilet. This apartment was part of a subdivided house and on day two I knocked on an adjoining door and asked the woman if they could possibly get me something for my stomach from a chemist. I had ventured out a little way, looking for one, but had to return to the apartment too quickly to make any discovery.

Not only did this kind person arrange for me to have some medicine from the chemist but, within an hour or so, my landlady arrived.

Nothing wrong with the communication system in this country!

Bringing me some soup, the landlady finished the washing of the sheets that I had soiled and then offered to drive me, the next day, to my departure at nearby Shannon Airport.

This small hamlet had no banks or ATMs and I had no money, so this lift to the airport was appreciated. The short deviation, to let me see the family castle ruins and a tavern with the name of a female member of the family on the front, was generously offered, as we made our way to the airport.

The landlady, knowing so many people at the airport, was off talking when I spotted an ATM. I could see her from there. She looked around in dismay as she imagined I was doing a runner, so I gave her a wave. I paid her for the accommodation, for the car hire and for her help, interest and care.

We said our goodbyes.

When I meet people from Ireland I tell them the story of how they had stolen an hour of my life. They respond with 'come back in October.'

My birthday is not in that month.

Lavinia Tarrant.

Bike

Beside the mulberry tree of a long ago Christmas, a bike leans against a black trunk, shines green and gold in summer light: the Malvern Star polished to almost new. An unseasonable dew falls this Christmas sunrise, the day just beginning to warm; shadows lengthen as the dream of riding slides silently away. From the house, father's voice calls girls in for tea.

Today the vines are in new leaf but the silences are still here, the mulberry trunk gnarled, shadowed by winter rain. These vines have grown for years – they are not new. Under a canopy of leaves and shaded from summer sun, two little girls sing songs of imaginings; weave the future in their hands.

In moving light, father's voice whispers, calls the girls in for tea.

Rose van Son

When Turner was here

some days it seems that Turner was here
overnight   tinting the walls / the sky
with brushes touching up
morning light   an estranged softness falls here.

As you look beyond the city skyline
you will see Turner's soft tones
—a touch of pink, a pastel blue
stretching to almost white
—a splash of grey, thicker
darker than you remember

But this is my sky, you will say
sky of late night early day
tinted by a raven's cry, black
caw piqued against grey
birds recalled   play
summer in the park

Rose van Son

Holidays = Work

I was born in England in 1934. My childhood memories of WWII are vividly clear. I was unwittingly witness to the necessity which emancipated women from their traditional roles. My female relatives discarded gloves and frilly hats for munition factory overalls and land girl khaki, became lorry drivers, mechanics and bus conductresses, and all – shockingly! – in trousers.

Society's eyes were opened to the wasted potential of women, so a post-war education initiative evolved to award scholarships in prestigious schools to impecunious but able female students. I won one of those places. But two years later, my father died suddenly: family decided I should follow my female relatives, leave school at fourteen and contribute to our finances.

However, my new world had opened "magic casements". Certainly was there also the memory of those emancipated war women. I could find a way out, work in the holidays and help my widowed mother.

So, "holidays" became synonymous with "work".

We lived in a semi-rural area, so part-time was easy to find in season. I did pea picking (eat as much as you like), cutting cabbages (huge leaves full of water after rain and wet feet), dig potatoes (drag a hessian sack through wet clay picking up cut and squashed tubers left behind the harvester).

I had a spell as an assistant at the January sales (learning some dodgy retail ploys there).

But the steepest learning curve was as temporary "postie" delivering Christmas mail. Fifteen was the minimum age to be taken on; it paid well, and I needed the money. I was directed to the

Central Post Office in the large Midlands city where I lived. Each temp was assigned to a regular postman to help deliver the enormous amounts of mail from the beginning of December until Christmas Eve.

Start time was 6am, to sort area mail into streets, each bundle held by a thick rubber band. My postie had a central area, densely populated in run-down housing. He, of course, gave me the poorest streets, often three families in one house, a huge load to carry in a canvas bag slung across the body. As skinny and boney as I was then, there was no way of carrying it comfortably. This was December, bitterly cold, snow melting into slush, shoes soaked, walking all the way. I had old leather shoes, worn thin in the sole; boots were unknown in those days.

Mail had to be put through slots in front doors after trudging up the path. If you've seen Onslow's house in "Keeping Up Appearances"... most of them were like that. Mail slots had a spring-hinged flap about 20cm long and 10 wide. Push it open with frozen fingers, try to manoeuvre a wad of cards in; some are too big, but you are not allowed to fold them; a dog inside snapping and barking, a hasty retreat, and a raucous voice shouting, "And close the gate." It's hanging on one hinge and dripping wet. After two hours, I am so cold I could cry. Then, shock! horror! Something is left in the bottom of the bag, cards out of order, two streets back and all uphill. You could lose the job for holding mail over until the next day.

The central library was on my round; I used to duck in there to thaw out, until I was spotted one day and docked a day's pay for 'dereliction of duty'. I never did Christmas mail again!

Even now that I have leisure and comfortable finances, I still cannot regard a 'holiday' as a rest period. It is a time to break new ground, gain some advantage; wasted if not productive.

'Holiday' in my mind is still spelled 'work'!

Astra Warren

An English Christmas

When I was a child in the Lake District in the North of England Christmas was a magical time. It started with me and my two brothers collecting holly berries to decorate the lounge. Dad hung them around pictures and a mirror on the walls where their red berries set the scene. Next came the tree, a real one in a big plant pot which we covered in red and green crepe paper. Under the tree Mum placed the Nativity scene with baby Jesus, surrounded with the animals and Mary and Joseph. The next exciting event was decorating the tree; there were lots of coloured baubles, tinsel, a fairy to sit on top, then Dad draped coloured lights around the tree. When he switched them on, there were ooh's and aah's. We made paper chains, hung them from the corners of the room to the centre.

Sometimes we had a white Christmas when it snowed. My brothers and I would wrap up in warm duffle coats, hats and scarves, run outside and have snowball fights, blowing on our fingers to warm them up. We made a snowman with a carrot for his nose, coal for his eyes and a twig for his mouth. Sometimes I would dress him in a beanie and scarf. We would take our toboggan into the field next to our house and have fun sliding down the hill, amid shrieks from us all. Mum used to put crumbs and fat out for the robin redbreast who I loved to see sitting on the windowsill.

The kitchen was the place to be at Christmas. Mum made plum pudding, Christmas cake, mince pies, rum butter and trifle. Delicious aromas wafted from the kitchen. She would give us the bowls to scrape out the last delicious morsels. We usually had a Goose for lunch, the plates groaning with roast potatoes and parsnips, fresh vegetables from dad's garden, home-made stuffing and mum's yummy gravy made with pan juices and vegetable water. Then the plum pudding which had three-penny bits hidden in it. A scream of delight when we found one in our serving. We were allowed to have a tiny drink of Port. A Christmas tradition when you paid someone a visit at Christmas was to be offered a glass of Port.

On Christmas eve we hung up one of dad's woollen socks at the bottom of the bed, tried to stay awake but always failed. We woke up to find the socks bulging with goodies; jumped out of bed with squeals of delight; started unpacking the sock. There was always a book, a box of chocolates, mine were "black magic" as I didn't like milk chocolate, still don't. Colouring books and pencils, an orange and apple, a couple of little novelties, a box of fruit jellies called Newberry Fruits. In the toe of the sock was half a crown.

I was taught to play the piano so at Christmas we always had a singalong to the Carols I played. I still love the Carols. In those winter months my brothers and I did big 1000 piece Jigsaws, played games like Ludo, Snakes and Ladders, and Dominoes.

At Christmas bells ring out, lights twinkle in shop windows and on trees. The spirit of Christmas is everywhere, people are kind to each other and smile. A time of celebration of family and friends, of giving and sharing. Let's try and make the spirit of Christmas last not just for the 12 days, but all the year round. The spirit of giving and sharing and being kind to each other.

Sheila Williamson

Holiday

England, Ireland, Scotland, Wales, France, Belgium, Greece – the holiday of a lifetime, a dream come true.

England abounds with history, castles, cathedrals and stately homes. I visit Warwick castle with its extensive grounds and medieval section, where I am asked by a staff member where I purchased my Fremantle leather hippy sandals. The Yorvik Viking Centre at York, a village re-enactment and replica of life in old England. The magnificent York Minster with intricate stained glass work and windows. The tower and Monks bar where Richard III was imprisoned.

Now we chug along on a steam train on the Yorkshire moors, the T.V. programme *Heartbeat* location. I visit the home of Shakespeare at Stratford-on-Avon, see the remains of a Roman fort, lead mines, abbeys and a watermill and wheel.

'The Pearl of the British Isles' is how the Lake District has been described. Stunning scenery, ten lakes, Windermere being the longest at ten miles with steamers and a ferry. A museum with the oldest mechanically powered boat in the world, *Dolly* 1850. Peaceful, relaxing waterfalls trickle down mountains, their peaks covered with mist. William Wordsworth wrote his poem *Daffodils* here, and said "It is the loveliest spot man hath ever found", and Beatrix Potter wrote her delightful animal stories enjoyed worldwide by children and adults. I walk down the garden path of *Hilltop*, her cottage which is now open to the public, and imagine Peter Rabbit scampering along.

She did her drawings from real animals that lived on the

property.

Coniston Lake where Donald Campbell's *Bluebird,* his self-built boat, disintegrated, killing him as he tried to break his own record. I enjoy the taste of freshwater salmon and trout in one of the many quaint pubs, warm and welcoming, full of character and good food.

Staffordshire in the Midlands: it is a summer night. I walk by the canal at 10.30 – it is still light. I notice the difference in the air and light here, not the same glare as back home. Earlier I watched two white swans with four baby cygnets swim past, and the canal folk who live on their boats as they hung out washing on their gaily painted decks.

Lichfield, home of the Lord and Earl of Lichfield: I wander round the cool interior of the cathedral, vast space to the ceiling, and imagine the organ playing. Sweet voices fill the empty air with songs of praise. I emerge into the bright sunlight to be greeted by Morris dancers as they swirl around in traditional dress of red and green; bells on their ankles tinkle merrily as they celebrate May and the coming of Spring. A crowd gathers, entranced by the spectacle.

The lovely old city of Chester, where we spend a day at the Zoological gardens. One of the biggest zoos, it is well worth a visit and runs as a Centre of Excellence for animal related education, welfare and above all conservation. The dream of George Mattershead, who wanted a zoo without bars.

Down the M6 motorway to London, we pass Woburn Abbey, Whipsnade Zoo, Luton and Victoria stations. The double decker tourist bus takes us to Buckingham Palace where Chinese and Japanese tourists push their cameras through the bars of the gates to film the changing of the guards. On to St. Paul's Cathedral, Houses of Parliament, Trafalgar Square, Oxford Street, Soho, Big Ben. Places that were just names are now coming alive. I view the magnificent paintings in the National Art Gallery. Edged with ornate gilt frames, some are so enormous it takes a crane to move them. We pass cyclists who wear masks, people asleep in cardboard boxes, a bag lady pushes a trolley and abuses everyone. London has it all, a great place to visit and see the shows, but expensive.

Aboard the Ffestiniog train in Wales we travel level with the treetops past pine plantations, slate mines, waterfalls, deer; on through the Snowdonia Ranges. The air is clean, the sheep look content. I love the lilting Welsh language with the hard to pronounce names, Tan-y-bwlch, Glan-y-pwll, Tanygrisiau. We visit Caernarfon Castle with its walled towers which have survived unbroken, about 800 yards of them.

Trainbound for Edinburgh, we pass lots of rabbits in the fields. It is a beautiful old city with an extinct volcano. I have my photo taken with a Scotsguard busker wearing a kilt, but am not brave enough to ask him what he wears underneath. Robert Louis Stevenson lived here as a child; Agatha Christie married here. We watch the changing of the guards at the castle, view the Scottish crown jewels and enter St. Mary's chapel, which is the highest point in the city. They are preparing for the Edinburgh Fringe Festival, a major event. We walk the Royal Mile to the Queen's Scottish residence, Holyrood House. The street is full of interesting shops, quaint cobblestone alleyways and Tartan Taxis.

We take advantage of the cheap fares to Greece to spend a week in the sun. Thassos, a paradise with sparkling emerald waters and white sands. Mountainous rocky dense forests of cedar, oak, chestnut and fir. Sleepy hamlets in mountain villages, where time stands still. Pure water runs over rocks; goats amble by with bells tinkling. An old lady in black leads a donkey and cart; silver olive trees, dark green pine used for making the local wine Retzina. Plums, walnuts, grapes and honey are cultivated. Corn, beans, tomatoes, potatoes and asparagus are grown. Perched high on a rock, Archangelo Monastery over-looks the sea.

Whitewashed houses with red terracotta roofs and marble floors. I learn the traditional dancing at a Bouzouki night, sample Retzina, fresh olives, feta cheese, Greek salad and tzatziki (the yummy cucumber, yoghurt and garlic dip). This is an island of history and myth, ancient stone ruins and marble mines. A week of complete relaxation.

South to Land's End, through Devon and Cornwall, across Dartmoor. I love the wild desolate moors, where badgers and foxes roam. Tiny moor ponies lick salt off the rocks. Breathtaking views of distant hills, capped with rocky outcrops. We stop for a glass of the local cider, Scrumpy. Princetown jail in the centre of the moors has an eerie feel. There are headstones of prisoners who escaped and perished in this unforgiving, harsh landscape. On to Jamaica Inn Museum and Smugglers Bar on Bodmin Moor. The quaint fishing port of Polperro, where pirates and smugglers came ashore long ago. No cars in the village, a stream runs through. I walk the narrow cobblestone streets past white-washed cottages with thatched roofs, a Blacksmith forge, and feel I have gone back in time. I enjoy a Devonshire tea with thick clotted cream and homemade strawberry jam.

On to Poldark mine, a heritage complex where they conduct mine tours, an air of mystery and suspense here. Finally to Penzance and Land's End, where I stand on the big rocks jutting out to sea on the bottom tip of England. From here there are day trips by air or sea to the Isles of Scilly.

I look back at the white chalk cliffs of Dover as we cross the English channel by ferry to France. We arrive at Calais, on to Dunkerque, rural and industrial, a farming area with lots of canals. The houses are small, the land very flat, would you believe we just passed McDonalds. A couple of hours drive, we are in Belgium, Bruges. We take a tour down the canal which runs through the city. Magnificent Flemish/Baroque architecture, cosmopolitan atmosphere, side walk cafes. The guide translates in four languages. Colourful parks and gardens, a special lane for cyclists, underground parking, cobble-stones, a friendly city. We ride in a horse and cart, sample Belgium chocolate, admire exquisite lace hanging in windows.

Driving back·up England we decide to stop at the ancient city of Avalon, Glastonbury. Here stand the ruins of a 13th century chapel where the last Abbot was hung, drawn and quartered. At the top of the Tor (a Celtic word for rocky hilltop) are spectacular views of sweeping plains, a powerful area steeped in legend.

The last stop on our holiday is Ireland: we drive through Wales to Holyhead in Anglesey to take the ferry over. The Irish roads are narrow with high hedges and wild fuchsia growing in profusion. Candlelit shrines and statues adorn the wayside, neat colourful houses with window boxes of stunning colours and blooms. There are potato sellers, gypsy camps with horses and dogs, washing hanging in trees. An old man sits outside a thatched farmhouse and tells me "God made time, then man made haste". Police are called *Garda* – money is *punce*; most places accept English currency.

In the foyer at Waterford Crystal stands an elaborate crystal Grandfather clock. Kilarney Lake looks like glass, still reflections of trees in its waters. We pass a goat leading a herd of cows. The Ring of Kerry has waterfalls, mountains, lakes and the sea: breath-taking scenery. Ireland is much more beautiful than I had imagined. We pass Viking ruins, a monastic 6th century site.

We stay at a farmhouse Bed and Breakfast where they serve black puddings and Irish soda bread. I am getting partial to Irish coffee. Underneath a tree on a plaque in the garden I read these words.

Kind hearts are the garden
Kind thoughts are the roots
Kind words are the blossoms
Kind deeds are the fruits.

Sheila Williamson

White Christmas

White Christmas lingers still
as tired snow slips from roofs and trees.
Branches bare and lonely reach for light,
and cows in farmyards look depressed.

As misty street lamps glow,
dismal clouds drift over town, and
weary footsteps trail damp pavements
quiet, in a damp cold world.

Memories pierce the absence
of long ago loved ones who gave
unasked their warm and loving company,
in days that were noisy and full.

Time gentles the silence of winter
while pale sunlight greets the snowdrops
pushing and clustering round cold trees
bringing the first sweet breath of spring.

Beryl Wincott

And Snow Began to fall

Winter skies looked down upon the cold and lonely trees.
Open fields bereft of flowers, dark and hidden seeds.
Shuttered houses kept warmth in as weary footstep trailed
The grey and empty pavements on this a gloomy day.

Frozen in celestial realms clouds were seen to form,
And being stirred by heaven's breath, snow began to fall.
Giant snowflakes tumbled down from white and silent skies,
Drifting high above the town and over countryside.

It softly fell on old tin sheds, on roofs and chimney pots,
on houses, hedgerows, fields and trees, on cars and lone bus stops.
The snow it fell so thickly on frozen ponds and reeds,
it buried gardens quickly and early springtime seeds

The dogs were chasing snowflakes along the misty lanes,
Making tracks with paw-prints and sniffing snowy trails.
They leapt and played with children catching sticks and balls,
running through the winter scene, when snow began to fall.

The shops in town were all ablaze with coloured lights and toys,
ribbons, cards and Christmas trees along the busy aisles.
People, warm in coats and scarves, sang in pure delight,
it's snowing and it's Christmas: we'll have Christmas that is white.

Beryl Wincott

Fallen Angel

(A Christmas story)

It was nearly midnight when Gabriella landed in the drift of snow near the coal shed.

Millie Perkins was still awake, but propped against the pillows and sipping Irish coffee. The bedroom was as cozy as an oven, tucked as it was under the thatched roof of her cottage.

If it hadn't been for Leonardo, who lifted his head and meowed, as he kneaded the eiderdown, she wouldn't have heard a thing. Reluctantly she slipped the book she was reading aside. She was fond of reading, especially romance, and didn't want to leave the hero in the middle of a crucial scene, where he was about to declare his undying love for the heroine.

She admitted to a twinge of alarm as she rose from her bed and slid into the sheepskin slippers her daughter had given her for Christmas. It had been naughty of her to open the gift in advance, but as she'd already guessed what the parcel contained, and taking into account that her current slippers were threadbare and trodden down at heel ... well she didn't see the point in waiting.

Not that anyone was there to tell her off. She'd be spending this Christmas alone in the little cottage she'd once shared with her husband, Frank. Her beloved granddaughter had gone into labour early and Millie was now waiting for news, thrilled to think the child might be born on Christmas day.

Twitching the curtain aside she peered into the garden. Not to be left out Leonardo pawed the crack in the curtain wider so he could satisfy his own curiosity.

Millie didn't see anything out of place, especially what she was looking for, a single set of footprints in the snow to signal an intruder. 'Good Heavens!' She jumped, when a small winged creature suddenly emerged from under the snow in a flurry of golden sparks. When they settled Millie saw that the little creature was glowing. It was also injured and crawled across the snow towards the cottage, dragging a wing behind her.

Leonardo rear-ended himself to the floor and took refuge under the bed, his yellow eyes peering out from the darkness.

'Don't be such a cowardy custard,' Millie said and she reached for her glasses. 'Goodness, I do believe it's a fairy.'

Millie was pleased. She'd believed in fairies ever since she was a child and her father had taken her to see *A Midsummer Night's Dream*, on stage. She believed in lots of odd things, ghosts, goblins, elves, and magic. She helped the squirrels by gathering acorns in the winter and she strung strings of suet, bacon rind and nuts within their reach.

As she explained to her daughter, it didn't hurt to give God's creatures a hand when they needed it.

She'd never expected to see a real fairy though, and was excited about it. What a wonderful tale she would have to tell her great grandchild.

Nevertheless she proceeded with caution. Snatching up the wooden spoon on the way through the kitchen she shuffled past the Christmas tree with its coloured lights and tinsel. The spoon wasn't much of a weapon but better than nothing and one couldn't be too careful these days.

The night cold was bitter and she jumped when the church bells struck eleven. Millie couldn't take her eyes off the fairy. She was a cute little thing with a fluttering movement and she would sit nicely on the top of her little Christmas tree. Leonardo had practised his cat skills on their previous tree and had chewed the fairy's wings off.

'Don't just stand there looking,' the creature said peevishly. 'If I don't get warm soon, I'll perish.'

Millie eyed the soft white shift the fairy wore. 'You do seem unsuitably clothed for this inclement weather,' and she lifted the creature into her shawl. 'You must allow me to look after you.'

'Don't hold me so tight; one of my wings is already damaged and if it doesn't heal I'll have some explaining to do.'

Millie retraced her steps and secured the door behind them. She placed her small charge in one of the sheepskin slippers. 'There, that's just the place for a fairy to sleep. I do hope you're one of the good fairies.'

The creature placed her hands on her hips and sizzled red sparks. 'A fairy? My name is Gabriella and I happen to be an angel, one of the cherub types. The last time I carried a VIP soul I miscalculated the landing, and they wouldn't take the fact that I'm dyslexic into account.'

Millie supposed the angel meant, a Very Important Person, but she didn't know who *they* were or what dyslexic meant. She hoped it wasn't infectious because she had the health of her own grandchild to consider. 'Goodness, that seems a bit harsh.'

Gabriella gazed around her in panic. 'Have you seen my soul bag? It had two souls left in it when I bounced off the tree.'

Millie found it lying in a puddle of blue pulsating light and felt quite comforted by it.

'I'm in a hurry.' Gabriella reminded her. 'So if you're going to help let's get on with it.'

'First, may I ask who this soul is for?'

'You may ask but that doesn't mean I'll answer. It's a precious little soul, destined to be a healer. This colour is extremely rare so it's in high demand. The infant should enter the host just before birth if it doesn't run out of energy first. But I need to rest before I continue with my journey.'

Millie felt anxious. 'My own great-grandchild is due to be born shortly.'

‘I know.’ Gabriella smiled as she took a mobile phone from her pocket and squinted at the screen. ‘It’s against the rules to tell you who my souls are intended for, but I can tell you I’ve got a female baby called Mary Saint.’ She clapped a tiny hand over her mouth when a roll of thunder grumbled overhead. ‘Holy Moses! Forget I said that.’

Millie tried to forget as she sewed the wing back on with the neat hemming stitches she’d learned as a child. The operation must have hurt but Gabriella didn’t make a sound, and Millie couldn’t help being a bit envious that the rare healing soul wasn’t destined for her own grandchild ... although she was pleased her grandchild was a girl.’

The angel looked low in energy. ‘I’ll have a rest then try to carry on and finish my journey.’

Millie suddenly had a brilliant idea. ‘Frank!’ she cried out.

‘Frank? I don’t understand. Who is Frank?’

‘My husband. He left me a motorbike and sidecar, one we went everywhere on when we were young.’ She’d kept the vehicle shining and clean but hadn’t been able part with it, not even when the vicar offered her more than it was worth.

Now Millie donned her leathers and goggles and tucked Gabriella into one of the sheepskin slippers so she’d be cosy and warm in the sidecar. She gently patted the tank of the elderly Triumph. ‘A life depends on you, Frankie.’

‘Hold tight and turn the ignition on else we won’t be going anywhere, old girl,’ Frank whispered, and Millie hoped she could remember how to drive it.

The handlebars wobbled as she put the bike into gear and she moved off in explosive leaps and splutters of smoke. Gradually the engine became a comforting, but rather noisy throb and by the time she cleared the village she’d gained some confidence and the bike some stability.

The roads were almost empty of people, the night air was cold.

Millie's fingers and toes were numb and her cheeks glowed like a couple of ripe tomatoes.

The vicar gazed at her in astonishment as Millie slowed down and waved her hand at him. She called out importantly as she rattled by, 'I'm on a mission of mercy and shouldn't be long.'

'I'm sure you are, Millie, but take care because the roads are icy ... and come and tell me all about it on your way back.'

They made good time but when they arrived at the hospital Gabriella seemed to be quite spiritless and a concerned Millie asked, 'Are you all right, my dear? You seem to have lost colour.'

Gabriella gave her a wan smile. One soul has lost its lustre and I'm trying to conserve the strength I have left so we should say good-bye now, Mrs Perkins. In case I can't get back try not to let anyone see you when you go to the nursery else they might try and stop you.'

When Millie realised why it was too late because Gabriella had gone.

In the distance came a peal of church bells, muted, but much louder than the local church bell. Goodness, they only gave the cathedral bells some exercise on very special occasions.

A star sped across the sky and hovered there for a moment till its light faded ... another angel delivering souls, perhaps? She decided to invite the vicar for breakfast so they could debate the subject.'

Perhaps some other time she reasoned and decided to pay a visit to her new grandchild first.

There were two babies in the nursery wing, both encased in plastic bubbles. The boy wore a blue beanie, the girl a pink one. Both were adorable and when Millie blew them a kiss her sweet granddaughter stretched and a pair of skinny legs hitched into the air. The boy blew a bubble. He had the looks of Millie's grandmother and that of her late husband, from his balding head right down to his skinny legs.

How odd that they resembled each other; they could be brother and sister,' she thought.

'A Very Important Pair,' she whispered, and she shivered. Was it a second coming from HIM! After all, it was Christmas, though she hadn't expected a personal visit. Surely, she wasn't that important.

She wasn't. Perhaps she had caught the Lexia germ from the angel.

A nurse bustled in and sent her packing with. 'How did you get in?'

'The angels guided my feet,' she said. 'The little girl is my great granddaughter. Her name is Millicent."

The nurse smiled. 'Five minutes then.

'She's going to make it,' Frank said against her ear as she made her escape. I don't know about the boy though.'

'He will grow into an honest lad with good morals.' Millie had seen the miracle herself, the most imperceptible stream of life that rippled through the frail body when Gabriella anointed the boy with the soul. When the light grew too bright for Millie's eyes she had to close them for a moment or two.'

Someone took her by the hand. It was Frank.

They watched together as the infant's erratic heartbeat steadied. For a moment Millie saw Gabriella reflected in the boy infant's eyes, and she smiled. 'Thank you, Gabriella.'

From the distance came the sound of the bells ringing. She had never heard them sound more joyous. If she hurried she could join the vicar and tell him where she'd been. Frank's old motorbike had served its purpose and it was time to give it a new lease on life.

She gave it to the vicar, when they were sipping a congratulatory glass of port and lemon in the kitchen, then when he'd gone Millie said to Leonardo, 'I had quite an adventure tonight.'

Someone giggled, and Millie was sure it was Gabriella.

Leonardo's eyes narrowed in on the Christmas tree and a red bauble fell and bounced across the floor. Leonardo was after it in a flash, playing it across the floor with the grace of a soccer star.

'Who would have guessed an angel would fall in my garden at Christmas?' Millie said to the vicar.

'And twin grandchildren as well, a very important pair indeed. You are blessed.'

Janet Woods

Other anthology titles by The Society of Women Writers WA Inc

Footprints
The Silver Collection
Strand of Pearls
Wild Women of the West
A Gift of Jade
A Taste of Childhook
Lest We Forget
Telling Tales
Life's Lessons Learnt

About
The Society of Women Writers WA Inc

The Society of Women Writers was first established in Australia in Sydney in September 1925, to bring together women writers and journalists in New South Wales. Their aims were to be a social body; to promote knowledge of literature; to encourage women writers; and to strengthen the ties of interest between Australian and visiting writers (www.womenwritersnsw.org/history/).

Until the 1970s, the Society was based in Sydney, using a postal critiquing system to keep in touch. During this decade, branches were established in other Australian states and the first Federal Constitution was adopted in 1978 with an agreement that Federal responsibility be transferred from state to state every two years. Twenty years later, the decision was made to decentralise, with each state forming its own Society.

The WA branch initially operated only through correspondence groups until the first President, Ethel Webb, was appointed in 1981 and members began to meet regularly. The Society of Women Writers WA was incorporated as an autonomous body on 25 February 2000.

Contact Details

The Society of Women Writers WA Inc
PO Box 434
Northbridge
Western Australia 6865
Tel: 0415 840 031
Email: swwofwa@gmail.com
Web: www.swwofwa.com.au